Jane Austen Junkie

get your fix!

A compilation of
over **600** books and **50** movies
inspired by Jane Austen

Susan J. Brown

For Sara, who helped with every step

CONTENTS

INTRODUCTION

Sometime from high school on I read the six full-length published Jane Austen novels. *Persuasion* was my favorite. I reread it every year or so and still swoon each time I get to Captain Wentworth's words, "You pierce my soul. I am half agony, half hope." I couldn't figure why *Pride and Prejudice* got all the play. Then several years ago over a long weekend in Pismo Beach, California, I reread *Pride and Prejudice* and could not put the book down! I fell in love with Elizabeth and Darcy. I wanted to be her and find him. Like many of you, I didn't want the book to end.

I was aware there were fan-written sequels but was happy with what I could imagine in my own mind. Then I came across one of the mysteries that features Jane Austen characters and decided to read it. After that I was hooked. I started looking for what else was out there and started reading. This was in the earlier days of self-publishing and many of the offerings were on individual author websites or self-publishing websites. I started keeping a list. After a while I reached a saturation point and moved on to other non-Jane Austen books.

Then recently my interest was sparked again and I took another look. I couldn't believe the explosion of Jane Austen-related works. At this point many are being published by mainstream publishers and e-readers have opened up a wider audience for these authors. The follow-ups are also attracting a new audience that may not have read Jane Austen's novels. I started doing more extensive research and at last count I had the following list of over 600 books and 50 movie adaptations inspired by Jane Austen and her works. If, like me, you're a voracious reader and avid Jane Austen fan, you often think "What will I read next?" This compilation in checklist format provides the answer.

METHODOLOGY

What's Included

- This book contains follow-ups to the six major published novels – *Emma, Mansfield Park, Northanger Abbey, Persuasion, Pride and Prejudice* and *Sense and Sensibility* plus works about Jane Austen herself and as a character.

- All books are English-language and most of the movies are too. Those movies not in English are available in some type of English-language version.

- The "author" may be an editor or compiler. Usually this is cleared up in the description.

- Descriptions are short for a quick scan. Most books are found on bookselling and review sites. More in-depth descriptions may be available through these sources.

What's Not Included

- This book does not include academic-type books, literary criticism or much biography. The non-fiction entries celebrate Jane Austen and contain information about her and her world.

- Stand-alone short stories and e-book only items. (A criteria change in 2012.)

It's Confusing

There are so many variations of these variations that it was hard to tell which copyright date and publisher and sometimes even title to use. I tried to use the information of the original publication so users may get a sense of when the book originally came out. For some books, there's an original self-published version then a more traditionally published one. For many of these, the title, publisher and date may be different. In these cases, I used the version available now.

How This Book is Organized

The Books

The first part of the book lists the over 600 follow-up books arranged alphabetically by Jane Austen novel title. Works of fiction appear first then works of non-fiction.

Fiction titles are arranged alphabetically by author within the categories listed below (not each title has works in each category).

- Prequels – books that take place before the events in the Jane Austen novel
- New Versions – new versions of the Jane Austen novel. Example, graphic novels
- Retellings – the events of the novel told in a different way. Includes what ifs, the story from a specific character's point of view and/or variations of the novel
- Sequels – stories that take place after the events of the Jane Austen novel
- Contemporary – modern day stories inspired by the Jane Austen novel

- Other – books that do not fit into the previous categories

Non-Fiction titles are arranged alphabetically by author and then in date order.

The Movies
The Movies are arranged in order of Jane Austen novel title then in date order.

For each movie, two actors' names are provided representing the following characters:

- Emma – Emma and Knightley
- Mansfield Park – Fanny and Edmund
- Northanger Abbey – Catherine and Henry
- Persuasion – Anne and Wentworth
- Pride and Prejudice – Elizabeth and Darcy
- Sense and Sensibility – Elinor and Marianne
- Jane Austen – two leads

A description is included when there is a different story than that of the Jane Austen novel and for the Jane Austen-based works.

EMMA

NEW VERSIONS

☐ Butler, Nancy and Lee, Janet
Emma
Marvel Illustrated
Marvel, 2011
A graphic novel version of *Emma*.

RETELLINGS

☐ Aiken, Joan
Jane Fairfax: The Secret Story of the Second Heroine in Jane Austen's Emma
St. Martin's Griffin, 1997
A retelling of the events of *Emma* focused on the relationship between Emma and Jane Fairfax.

☐ Austen-Leigh, Joan
A Visit to Highbury/Another View of Emma (also published as *Mrs. Goddard, Mistress of a School*)
St. Martin's Press, 1995
A retelling of *Emma* through correspondence between headmistress Mary Goddard and her sister, Charlotte Pinkney.

☐ Cornthwaite, Barbara
George Knightley, Esquire: Charity Envieth Not
CreateSpace, 2009
A retelling of *Emma* from Knightley's perspective.

☐ Cornthwaite, Barbara
George Knightley, Esquire: Lend Me Leave
CreateSpace, 2011
A follow-up to *Charity Envieth Not*.

☐ Delman, Joan Ellen
Lovers' Perjuries: Or, the Clandestine Courtship of Jane Fairfax and Frank Churchill
Joan Ellen Delman, 2007
A retelling focused on Jane and Frank and their courtship and engagement.

☐ Grange, Amanda
Mr. Knightley's Diary
Berkley Trade, 2007
This book retells *Emma* from Mr. Knightley's perspective.

☐ Greensmith, Jane
Imitations of Austen
Lulu.com, 2008
A collection of short stories that includes backstories, sequels and what-ifs to Austen's novels.

☐ Grey, Charlotte
The Journal of Miss Jane Fairfax
Robert Hale, 1983
An old diary is discovered in which Jane recounts her life from her days in Highbury, her upbringing by the Campbells and her relationships with Frank Churchill and Emma.

☐ Josephson, Wayne
Emma and the Vampires
Sourcebooks Landmark, 2010
A vampire adaptation of *Emma*.

☐ Nattress, Laurel Ann
Jane Austen Made Me Do It: Original Stories Inspired by Literature's Most Astute Observer of the Human Heart
Ballantine Books, 2011
A collection of short stories inspired by Jane Austen and her works.

☐ Rann, Adam
Emma and the Werewolves: Jane Austen's Classic Novel with Blood-Curdling Lycanthropy
Coscom Entertainment, 2009
A werewolf-filled version of *Emma*.

☐ Royde-Smith, Naomi
Jane Fairfax
Macmillan, 1940
This novel is written in three books and focuses on the Campbells. It starts with Jane Fairfax as a child and continues through the events of *Emma*.

SEQUELS

☐ Austen-Leigh, Joan
Later Days at Highbury
St. Martin's Press, 1996
This novel takes up after the conclusion of *Emma* and focuses on the schoolmistress, Mrs. Goddard.

☐ Billington, Rachel
Emma & Knightley: Perfect Happiness in Highbury
Sourcebooks Landmark, 2008
One year after the conclusion of *Emma*, Emma and Knightley are living at Hartfield and interacting with the Westons, the Eltons and the Bateses. Problems arise as Knightley is tried by Emma's whims, Frank Churchill and events in his brother's family.

☐ Birchall, Diana
Mrs. Elton in America
Egerton House Publishing, 2004
This collection of three shorter works, "The Courtship of Mrs. Elton," "In Defense of Mrs. Elton" and "Mrs. Elton in America," covers the Eltons' courtship, her actions in Highbury and her adventures in America.

☑ Brinton, Sybil G.
Old Friends and New Fancies: An Imaginary Sequel to the Novels of Jane Austen
Unknown, 1913
Considered the first Jane Austen fan-fiction story conceived, the author takes characters from all of Jane Austen's novels and weaves them into a "concluding" story.

☐ Finn, Brenda
Anna Weston
Hedera Books, 2000
This is a sequel to *Emma*.

☐ Gillespie, Jane
Aunt Celia
St. Martin's Press, 1991
This sequel focuses on Celia Weston, the daughter of Mr. Weston and Miss Taylor and Stella Churchill, the daughter of Frank Churchill and Jane Fairfax.

☐ Gillespie, Jane
Truth and Rumor
Ulverscroft Large Print, 1995
This book takes place twenty years after the end of *Emma* and focuses on the Eltons and the Martins and their children.

☐ Kaye-Smith, Sheila and Stern, G.B.
More Talk of Jane Austen
Cassell, 1950
This book includes speculation about the lives of those in Jane Austen's six complete novels.

☐ Tennant, Emma
Emma in Love
Fourth Estate, 1997
This sequel picks up four years after the conclusion of *Emma* when a bored Emma again takes up matchmaking.

☐ Unknown
Gambles and Gambols: A Visit with Old Friends
Shelter Cove, 1983
This book is a *Mansfield Park* sequel that focuses
on Edmund's advancement in the church and
Fanny's search for a wife for Tom. Also included
are characters from *Pride and Prejudice, Emma and
Persuasion.*

CONTEMPORARY

☑ Archer, Juliet
The Importance of Being Emma
Choc Lit, 2008
Emma is a marketing director, Harriet is her
personal assistant and Mark Knightley runs
Donwell Organics. The story is told by both Emma
and Mark.

☐ Day, Summer
Pride & Princesses
CreateSpace, 2012
A contemporary young adult novel in which *Pride
and Prejudice meets Emma.*

☐ Rushton, Rosie
Secret Schemes & Daring Dreams
Jane Austen in 21st Century
Piccadilly Press, 2008
Emma's friend George needs help at his country
hotel so Emma arranges for Harriet to work there.

☐ Smith, Debra White
Amanda
The Austen Series
Harvest House, 2006
A contemporary Christian retelling in which a bored Amanda spruces up Haley with the idea of matching her with the local pastor. Unfortunately, Haley is dating Roger and the pastor is seeing someone else so Amanda switches her focus.

OTHER

☐ Brooke-Rose, Christine
Textermination
New Directions, 1992
Does not follow the plot of *Emma* but finds her, among other fictional characters, at a literary criticism conference.

☐ Hill, Reginald
There are no Ghosts in the Soviet Union
Avon Books, 1989
Included in this collection of short murder mysteries is "Poor Emma," a send-up of Jane Austen's style representing the upper class.

NON-FICTION

☐ Birtwistle, Sue and Conklin, Susie
The Making of Jane Austen's Emma
Penguin Books, 1996
Describes how the BBC transformed *Emma* into a television drama.

☐ Hendricks, Donald
Jane Austen's Emma: A Paper Doll
True Collectibles, 2000
This book includes a paper doll and clothes inspired by Emma.

MANSFIELD PARK

RETELLINGS

☐ Allen, Dorothy and Owen, Ann
Mansfield Park: An Alternative Ending
Kay and Douglas, Coventry, 1989
An alternate ending to *Mansfield Park* in which
alliances are shifted and Henry and Mary are
redeemed.

☐ Grange, Amanda
Edmund Bertram's Diary
Berkley Trade, 2008
This book retells the story of *Mansfield Park* from
Edmund Bertram's perspective.

☐ Greensmith, Jane
Imitations of Austen
Lulu.com, 2008
A collection of short stories that includes
backstories, sequels and what-ifs to Austen's novels.

☐ Nattress, Laurel Ann
*Jane Austen Made Me Do It: Original Stories Inspired by
Literature's Most Astute Observer of the Human Heart*
Ballantine Books, 2011
A collection of short stories inspired by Jane
Austen and her works.

☐ Nazarian, Vera
*Mansfield Park and Mummies: Monster Mayhem,
Matrimony, Ancient Curses, True Love, and Other Dire
Delights*
Curiosities, 2009
A story set in ancient Egypt that is a romantic
monster adaptation of *Mansfield Park*.

☐ Shepherd, Lynn
Murder at Mansfield Park
St. Martin's Griffin, 2010
Mary Crawford plays detective when Fanny turns
up dead.

☐   Terry, Judith
Miss Abigail's Part, or Version and Diversion
Gage Distribution, 1986
A retelling of *Mansfield Park* from a maid's point of view. It focuses on Henry Crawford and Maria and Julia Bertram.

SEQUELS

☐   Aiken, Joan
Mansfield Revisited: A Jane Austen Entertainment
Indigo, 1996
Fanny Price has married Edmund Bertram and they have left for the Caribbean. Fanny's sister Susan arrives at Mansfield Park as Lady Bertram's new companion and meets the Crawfords.

☑   Aiken, Joan
The Youngest Miss Ward
St. Martin's Press, 1998
A sequel that focuses on the Ward sisters and a newly created character - a younger sister.

☐   Aiken, Joan
Mansfield Park Revisited
Sourcebooks Landmark, 2008
This book is a sequel to *Mansfield Park*.

☐   Atchia, Paula
Mansfield Letters
Trans-Atlantic Publications, 1996
A sequel to *Mansfield Park*.

☑ Brinton, Sybil G.
Old Friends and New Fancies: An Imaginary Sequel to the Novels of Jane Austen
Unknown, 1913
Considered the first Jane Austen fan-fiction story conceived, the author takes characters from all of Jane Austen's novels and weaves them into a "concluding" story.

☐ Brown, Francis
Susan Price, or Resolution
John Lane, 1929
This book is a sequel to *Mansfield Park*.

☐ CI, Victoria
A More Prosperous Trial of the State
Lulu.com, 2007
This sequel picks up a couple of months after Elizabeth's and Darcy's wedding and focuses on Caroline Bingley and her suitors. It also brings in characters from *Mansfield Park*.

☐ Gillespie, Jane
Ladysmead
St. Martin's Press, 1983
A sequel to *Mansfield Park*.

☐ Gillespie, Jane
The Reluctant Baronet
Thorndike Press, 1999
This novel follows Tom Bertram's story as he administers his father's estates.

☐ Gordon, Victor
Mrs. Rushworth
Andre Deutsch, 1990
This book is a sequel to *Mansfield Park*.

☐ Kaye-Smith, Sheila and Stern, G.B.
More Talk of Jane Austen
Cassell, 1950
This book includes speculation about the lives of those in Jane Austen's six complete novels.

☐ Unknown
Gambles and Gambols: A Visit with Old Friends
Shelter Cove, 1983
This book focuses on Edmund's advancement in the church and Fanny's search for a wife for Tom. Also included are characters from *Pride and Prejudice, Emma and Persuasion.*

CONTEMPORARY

☐ Smith, Debra White
Central Park
The Austen Series
Harvest House, 2005
In this contemporary Christian version, Francine moves in with her aunt and uncle in New York City and forms a bond with their foster son, Ethan. When Ethan introduces Carrie and her brother Hugh, Francine senses danger.

NON-FICTION

☐ Chandler, Steve and Hill, Terrence N.
Two Guys Read Jane Austen
Robert Reed Publishers, 2008
The two guys take on *Pride and Prejudice* and *Mansfield Park,* reading and commenting on her novels and digressing into music, sports, and history.

☐ Hendricks, Donald
Fanny, Jane Austen's Mansfield Park: A Paper Doll
True Collectibles, 2000
This book includes a paper doll and clothes inspired by Fanny.

NORTHANGER ABBEY

NEW VERSION

☐ Butler, Nancy and Lee, Janet
Northanger Abbey #1
Marvel, 2011
A graphic novel version of *Northanger Abbey*.

☐ Hajeski, Nancy
Northanger Abbey #2
Marvel, 2011
A graphic novel version of *Northanger Abbey*.

RETELLINGS

☐ Grange, Amanda
Henry Tilney's Diary
Berkley Trade, 2011
A retelling of *Northanger Abbey* from Henry Tilney's
perspective.

☐ Greensmith, Jane
Imitations of Austen
Lulu.com, 2008
A collection of short stories that includes
backstories, sequels and what-ifs to Austen's novels.

☐ Nattress, Laurel Ann
*Jane Austen Made Me Do It: Original Stories Inspired by
Literature's Most Astute Observer of the Human Heart*
Ballantine Books, 2011
A collection of short stories inspired by Jane
Austen and her works.

☐ Nazarian, Vera
Northanger Abbey and Angels and Dragons
Curiosities, 2010
Dragons, angels and gothic horror are present in
this adaptation of *Northanger Abbey*.

SEQUELS

☑ Brinton, Sybil G.
Old Friends and New Fancies: An Imaginary Sequel to the Novels of Jane Austen
Unknown, 1913
Considered the first Jane Austen fan-fiction story conceived, the author takes characters from all of Jane Austen's novels and weaves them into a "concluding" story.

☐ Gillespie, Jane
Uninvited Guests
Janus Publishing, 1994
This book is a sequel to *Northanger Abbey*.

☐ Kaye-Smith, Sheila and Stern, G.B.
More Talk of Jane Austen
Cassell, 1950
This book includes speculation about the lives of those in Jane Austen's six complete novels.

☐ Sullivan, Margaret C.
There must be Murder
LibriFiles Publishing, 2010
A sequel to *Northanger Abbey* that focuses on Catherine and Henry who, three months after their marriage, are involved in a mystery.

CONTEMPORARY

☐ James, Jenni
Northanger Alibi
The Jane Austen Diaries
Brigham Distributing, 2012
While visiting Seattle, Claire meets Tony Russo and is convinced he is a vampire.

☐ Rushton, Rosie
Summer of Secrets
Jane Austen in 21st Century
Piccadilly Press, 2007
Caitlin Morland wins an art scholarship to Mulberry
Court College. There she is befriended by Izzy
Thorpe and Summer Tilney and falls for Summer's
brother.

☐ Shealy, Carissa
Norfanger Plantation
CreateSpace, 2010
A vampire-inspired version of *Northanger Abbey*.

☐ Smith, Debra White
Northpointe Chalet
The Austen Series
Harvest House, 2005
This book is a contemporary Christian version of
Northanger Abbey in which Kathy Moore opens a
coffee shop in small town Colorado.

NON-FICTION

☐ Hendricks, Donald
Catherine, Jane Austen's Northanger Abbey: A Paper Doll
True Collectibles, 2000
This book includes a paper doll and clothes
inspired by Catherine.

PERSUASION

RETELLINGS

☐ Beckford, Grania
Virtues & Vices: A Delectable Rondelet of Love and Lust in Edwardian Times
St. Martin's Press, 1981
An "adult" retelling of *Persuasion* featuring Sir Wilfrid Elliott of Kellynch Hall and his neighbor, Lady Veronica Russell.

☐ Grange, Amanda
Captain Wentworth's Diary
Berkley Trade, 2008
This book retells the story of *Persuasion* from Captain Wentworth's perspective.

☐ Greensmith, Jane
Imitations of Austen
Lulu.com, 2008
A collection of short stories that includes backstories, sequels and what-ifs to Austen's novels.

☐ Jeffers, Regina
Captain Wentworth's Persuasion (also published as *Wayward Love: Captain Frederick Wentworth's Story*)
Ulysses Press, 2010
A retelling of *Persuasion* from Captain Wentworth's perspective.

☑ Kaye, Susan
None but You
Frederick Wentworth, Captain
Wytherngate Press, 2007
This book retells the story of *Persuasion* from Captain Wentworth's perspective up to the point of the group's visit to Lyme.

☑ Kaye, Susan
For You Alone
Frederick Wentworth, Captain
Wytherngate Press, 2008
This book retells the story of *Persuasion* from
Captain Wentworth's perspective and starts with the
group in Lyme.

☐ Kaye, Susan
Shadows in a Brilliant Life
Poppycock Press, 2011
Captain Frederick Wentworth is not an honorable
man and Louisa Musgrove is the object of his lust.
Anne must stop him from ruining Louisa.

☐ Kaye, Susan
When I Dream, I Have You
Poppycock Press, 2011
What if the second meeting of Captain Wentworth
and Anne was postponed by just a few months?
What a difference a little time can make.

☐ Kaye, Susan
The Little Particulars of the Circumstance
Poppycock Press, 2011
What if Anne and Captain Wentworth are
quarantined together? Will they overcome their hurt
and reunite?

☐ Menzies, June
His Cunning or Hers
Jane Austen Society of North America, 1993
Letters to, from and between characters in
Persuasion.

☐ Nattress, Laurel Ann
Jane Austen Made Me Do It: Original Stories Inspired by Literature's Most Astute Observer of the Human Heart
Ballantine Books, 2011
A collection of short stories inspired by Jane Austen and her works.

☐ Simonsen, Mary Lydon
Anne Elliot, a New Beginning
CreateSpace, 2010
This retelling has Anne Elliott feeling liberated by her spinster status, becoming a long distance runner then reuniting with Wentworth.

☐ Simonsen, Mary Lydon
Captain Wentworth Home from the Sea
Quail Creek Publishing, 2011
When Captain Wentworth returned to the sea, he hoped to leave memories of Anne behind but is unable to until an accident takes his memory. When he once again meets Anne he remembers nothing of their previous engagement.

SEQUELS

☐ Baker, Helen
Connivance
Lulu.com, 2008
The story of Mrs. Clay after the conclusion of *Persuasion*.

☑ Brinton, Sybil G.
Old Friends and New Fancies: An Imaginary Sequel to the Novels of Jane Austen
Unknown, 1913
Considered the first Jane Austen fan-fiction story conceived, the author takes characters from all of Jane Austen's novels and weaves them into a "concluding" story.

☐ Figueroa, Timothy
The Lady Anne Elliot Wentworth, Duchess of Glastonbury
Timothy Figueroa, 2011
A sequel to *Persuasion* that spans Anne's life from accepting Captain Wentworth proposal to her death.

☐ Gillespie, Jane
Sir Willy
Robert Hale, 1992
This sequel to *Persuasion* focuses on Mrs. Clay's two daughters.

☐ Hile, Laura
Mercy's Embrace: Elizabeth Elliot's Story Book 1 - So Rough a Course
Wytherngate Press, 2009
A sequel to *Persuasion* focused on Elizabeth Elliott.

☐ Hile, Laura
Mercy's Embrace: Elizabeth Elliot's Story Book 2 - So Lively a Chase
Wytherngate Press, 2009
A follow-up to *So Rough a Course*.

☐ Hile, Laura
Mercy's Embrace: Elizabeth Elliot's Story Book 3 - The Lady Must Decide
Wytherngate Press, 2010
A follow-up to *So Lively a Chase*.

☐ Honour, MO
Anne Nee Elliott from Where Jane Austen Left Off
Unknown, Unknown
No information is available on this book.

☐ Kaye-Smith, Sheila and Stern, G.B.
More Talk of Jane Austen
Cassell, 1950
This book includes speculation about the lives of those in Jane Austen's six complete novels.

☐ Unknown
Gambles and Gambols: A Visit with Old Friends
Shelter Cove, 1983
This book is a *Mansfield Park* sequel that focuses on Edmund's advancement in the church and Fanny's search for a wife for Tom. Also included are characters from *Pride and Prejudice*, *Emma* and *Persuasion*.

CONTEMPORARY

☑ Archer, Juliet
Persuade Me
Choc Lit, 2011
Anna Elliott regrets giving up Rick Wentworth. Now he's back but has trouble with "forgive and forget."

☐ Balogh, Mary, et al
Bespelling Jane Austen
HQN Books, 2011
Four novellas by different authors offer paranormal spins to Jane Austen's works.

☐ Cohen, Paula Marantz
Jane Austen in Scarsdale: Or Love, Death and the SATs
St. Martin's Griffin, 2007
Anne Ehrlich breaks up with poor boyfriend Ben Cutler. Years later when Anne is working as a high school guidance counselor, Ben, now well-to-do, reenters her life.

☐ Cox, Karen M.
Find Wonder in all Things
Meryton Press, 2012
James is ready for a future with Laurel but she ends things. When reunited years later, will their spark reignite?

☐ Fielding, Helen
Bridget Jones: The Edge of Unreason
Penguin Books, 2004
Four weeks after the end of *Bridget Jones's Diary*, this book follows Bridget's up and down relationship with Mark Darcy.

☐ Horowitz, Laurie
The Family Fortune
Harper Paperbacks, 2007
Jane Fortune ends her relationship with writer Max Wellman who received a fellowship sponsored by her family's foundation. Max becomes successful while Jane runs the foundation and endures her family who has to rent out their Beacon Hill home.

☐ James, Jenni
Persuaded
The Jane Austen Diaries
Walnut Springs Press, 2012
Years ago, Amanda let her friends persuade her to break up with Will because they thought he was a loser. Now he's back and better than ever. Will he take Amanda back?

☐ Kiely, Tracy
Murder Most Persuasive
Minotaur Books, 2011
When the pool at Elizabeth Parker's great-uncle
Martin Reynolds' house is dug up, a dead body
is discovered. Detective Joe Muldoon is the
investigator and one-time boyfriend of Elizabeth's
cousin Ann who was persuaded to end the
relationship with him.

☐ Nathan, Melissa
Persuading Annie
William Morrow Paperbacks, 2004
Annie Markham, at 19, ended her relationship with
Jake Mead after being persuaded by her godmother
Susannah. Seven years later, Annie's family business
needs help and Susannah hires Jake as a consultant
to rescue it.

☐ Odiwe, Jane
Searching for Captain Wentworth
Paintbox Publishing, 2012
Sophie stays in the house next to Jane Austen's in
Bath where she finds a glove that transports her
to Regency times where she meets her Captain
Wentworth.

☐ Reynolds, Abigail
Morning Light
The Woods Hole Quartet
Interdial Press, 2011
The best friend of Annie's late husband left the
country in order to avoid seeing Annie marry
another man. This is the story of his return.

☐ Rushton, Rosie
Echoes of Love
Jane Austen in 21st Century
Piccadilly Press, 2010
Anna adored Felix Wentworth but called off their relationship. Two years later, he's home from Afghanistan. Anna wants him back but will he give her a second chance?

☐ Saunders, Kaitlin
A Modern Day Persuasion
BookSurge Publishing, 2011
Anne ended things with fiance Rick. A decade later she's still single and struggling financially. Rick reenters her life at the same time as a new beau.

☐ Siplin, Karen
Such a Girl
Washington Square Press, 2005
Kendall and Jack met and fell in love. Kendall broke up with him and went on to work in a New York hotel. Jack, who has since started a successful brewery, reappears in Kendall's life.

☐ Smith, Debra White
Possibilities
The Austen Series
Harvest House, 2006
This contemporary Christian version of *Persuasion* features Allie Ellen and Frederick Wently who plans to join the Air Force. They fall in love but Allie is persuaded by her aunt to not pursue the relationship.

OTHER

☐ Measham, Donald
Jane Austen and the Polite Puzzle
Lulu.com, 2007
Young Jane Austen plays a card game and involves readers in a discovery as they see the game reenacted by Regency young ladies and their governesses. *Pride and Prejudice* and *Persuasion* are presented in social and historical context.

NON-FICTION

☐ Hendricks, Donald
Anne, Jane Austen's Persuasion: A Paper Doll
True Collectibles, 2000
This book includes a paper doll and clothes inspired by Anne.

PRIDE AND PREJUDICE

PREQUELS

☐ Aidan, Pamela
Young Master Darcy: A Lesson in Honour
Wytherngate Press, 2010
A prequel focused on Darcy at age 13, around the time of his mother's death.

☐ Grace, Maria
Darcy's Decision: Given Good Principles, Volume 1
Good Principles Publishing, 2011
This prequel takes place six months after the death of Darcy's father and depicts Darcy dealing with grief and learning who to trust.

☑ Hockensmith, Steve and Arrasmith, Patrick
Pride and Prejudice and Zombies: Dawn of the Dreadfuls
Quirk Books, 2010
A prequel that takes place four years before *Pride and Prejudice and Zombies*. The Bennet sisters are enjoying their peaceful country life until a funeral goes horribly wrong.

☐ Warren, Kate
The Bennets: A Pride and Prejudice Prequel
Lulu.com, 2006
This prequel explores how Mr. and Mrs. Bennet came to be together.

☐ Waters, Jeanne
Vanity and Verity
Unknown, 2011
A prequel that focuses on the society debuts of sisters Lady Anne and Lady Catherine Fitzwilliam.

NEW VERSIONS

Adams, Jennifer and Oliver, Allison
Pride & Prejudice: A BabyLit Board Book
Gibbs Smith, 2011
Pride and Prejudice simplified and illustrated for child readers.

Butler, Nancy and Petrus, Hugo
Pride and Prejudice
Marvel Classics
Marvel, 2010
A graphic novel version of *Pride and Prejudice*.

☐ Field, Alex
Mr. Darcy
New Frontier Publishing, 2011
A children's book that retells *Pride and Prejudice* and features cartoon ducks as the characters.

☐ Wang, Jack and Wang, Holman
Pride and Prejudice
Simply Read Books, 2012
A children's book that retells *Pride and Prejudice* in twelve words illustrated with felted characters.

RETELLINGS

☐ Adams, Alexa
First Impressions: A Tale of Less Pride & Prejudice
Outskirts Press, 2010
What happens if Mr. Darcy never speaks disdainfully of Elizabeth at the Meryton dance?

☐ Adriani, Susan
The Truth about Mr. Darcy (also published as *Affinity and Affection*)
Lossin Press, 2009
What if Darcy had not ridden away when he saw Wickham for the first time in Meryton and instead warned Elizabeth about him?

☑ Aidan, Pamela
An Assembly Such as This
Fitzwilliam Darcy, Gentleman
Touchstone, 2006
A retelling of *Pride and Prejudice* from Darcy's perspective. First of a trilogy.

☑ Aidan, Pamela
Duty and Desire
Fitzwilliam Darcy, Gentleman
Touchstone, 2006
A retelling of *Pride and Prejudice* from Darcy's perspective. Second of a trilogy.

☑ Aidan, Pamela
These Three Remain
Fitzwilliam Darcy, Gentleman
Touchstone, 2007
A retelling of *Pride and Prejudice* from Darcy's perspective. Third of a trilogy.

☐ Angell, Lavinia
The Sheik of Araby: Pride and Prejudice in the Desert
CreateSpace, 2010
While traveling in Algiers, Elizabeth is taken from her group and delivered into the hands of a Sheik. Could he be her Mr. Darcy?

☐ Armstrong, Amy
Pride and Prejudice
Total-E-Bound Publishing, 2012
A retelling of the *Pride and Prejudice* story with
electrifying sexual tension and heated glances.

☐ Avery, Aimee, Williams, June and Wilson, Enid
*Honor and Integrity: A Collection of Pride and Prejudice-
Inspired Short Stories* (Volume 1)
CreateSpace, 2012
A collection of nine stories covering Regency,
fantasy and modern genres.

☑ Aylmer, Janet
Darcy's Story
William Morrow Paperbacks, 2006
A retelling of *Pride and Prejudice* from Darcy's
perspective.

☐ Aylmer, Janet
Dialogue With Darcy
Copperfield Books, 2010
A continuation of *Darcy's Story*.

☐ Baxley, M.K.
The Mistress's Black Veil: A Pride and Prejudice
Vagary
CreateSpace, 2011
What if Lydia Bennet had gone to Brighton
while Elizabeth was visiting Charlotte at Rosings?
While searching for Lydia in London, Mr. Bennet
succumbs to a cold and subsequently dies of heart
failure. This book begins five years after these
events take place.

☐ Carlson, C. Rafe
An Unpleasant Walk
C. Rafe Carlson, 2011
Elizabeth becomes the mistress of Colonel
Fitzwilliam.

☐ Cecil, Amy
Pride and Prejudice, a Royal Disposition
CreateSpace, 2012
What if Elizabeth outranked Darcy?

☐ Childers, Casey
Twilight of the Abyss
CreateSpace, 2010
Elizabeth and Darcy meet in Hertfordshire, do not
insult each other and fall in love.

☐ Christie, Kate
Gay Pride & Prejudice
Second Growth Books, 2012
A gay and lesbian reinterpretation of *Pride
and Prejudice*. Netherfield Hall has been let by
a single man but he is not desirous of female
companionship.

☐ Cole, Barbara Tiller
*Fitzwilliam Ebenezer Darcy: Pride and Prejudice Meets a
Christmas Carol*
CreateSpace, 2011
This Jane Austen/Charles Dickens crossover story
features Fitzwilliam Ebenezer Darcy as a pitiful,
self-loathing, angst-ridden man who has lost the
chance to marry Elizabeth.

☐ Croft, J. Marie
Mr. Darcy Takes the Plunge
Rhemalda Publishing, 2010
What if Elizabeth and Jane, who have befriended
Georgiana and Anna Darcy, first encounter Mr.
Darcy after he swims in the pond at Pemberley?

☐ Dixon, PO
To Have His Cake (and Eat It Too): Mr. Darcy's Tale
CreateSpace, 2010
From Darcy's perspective, what if he had met
Elizabeth who is in diminished circumstances after
the death of her father?

☐ Dixon, PO
What He Would Not Do: Mr. Darcy's Tale Continues
CreateSpace, 2011
A follow-up to *To Have His Cake.*

☐ Dixon, PO
He Taught Me to Hope: Darcy and the Young Knight's Quest
CreateSpace, 2011
What if Elizabeth had been promised to another
man when she met Mr. Darcy?

☐ Dixon, PO
Still a Young Man: Darcy is in Love
CreateSpace, 2011
An older, widowed Elizabeth captivates a younger
Mr. Darcy.

☐ Dixon, PO
Bewitched, Body and Soul: Miss Elizabeth Bennet
CreateSpace, 2012
Elizabeth defies convention and decorum in an
attempt to
reunite her sister with the man she loves. She must
also forgive the man who dashed her sister's hopes.

☐ Dixon, PO
Matter of Trust: The Shades of Pemberly
CreateSpace, 2012
What if Wickham was of Darcy lineage rather than
the son of the steward?

☑ Edwards, John
Mr. Darcy's First Elizabeth
Unknown, 2012
As a young man, Darcy met another Elizabeth
who was his model for the woman he would marry.
When he meets Elizabeth Bennet, he asks the
original Elizabeth for advice.

☐ Fasman, Marjorie
The Diary of Henry Fitzwilliam Darcy
New Leaf Press, 1997
A retelling of *Pride and Prejudice* from Darcy's
perspective.

☐ Foster, Jeanne Desautel
Pride & Prejudice: Mary's Story
Sycamore Books, 2010
A retelling from Mary's perspective.

☐ Fuentes-Montero, Maria Elena
I Think of You
CreateSpace, 2012
Elizabeth is brilliant and due to childhood
memories doesn't think she'll marry - until she
meets Darcy.

☐ Grace, Maria
The Future Mrs. Darcy
Given Good Principles Volume 2
Good Principles Publishing, 2012
The Bennets are being cut from Meryton society
due to the behavior of the younger daughters. It's
up to Elizabeth to save the family's reputation.

☑ Grahame-Smith, Seth
Pride and Prejudice and Zombies
Quirk Books, 2009
This book includes original text of *Pride and Prejudice* with new zombie action scenes. A plague fells Meryton residents who begin returning from the dead. Elizabeth works to wipe out the zombie menace but gets distracted when Darcy arrives.

☐ Grahame-Smith, Seth, Lee, Tony and Richards, Cliff
Pride and Prejudice and Zombies: The Graphic Novel
Del Rey, 2010
Graphic novel version of *Pride and Prejudice and Zombies*.

☑ Grange, Amanda
Mr. Darcy's Diary
Sourcebooks Landmark, 2007
This book is a retelling of *Pride and Prejudice* from Darcy's perspective.

☐ Grange, Amanda
Wickham's Diary
Sourcebooks Landmark, 2011
This book is a retelling of *Pride and Prejudice* from Wickham's perspective.

☐ Grange, Amanda
Dear Mr. Darcy
Berkley Trade, 2012
A retelling of *Pride and Prejudice* from Darcy's perspective that begins with the death of his father.

☐ Greensmith, Jane
Imitations of Austen
Lulu.com, 2008
A collection of short stories that includes
backstories, sequels and what-ifs to Austen's novels.

☐ Hahn, Jan
An Arranged Marriage
Meryton Press, 2011
Elizabeth is forced into an arranged marriage with
Mr. Darcy after her father dies and leaves her with
few options.

☐ Hahn, Jan
The Journey
Meryton Press, 2011
After the Netherfield Ball, the carriage carrying
Elizabeth, Darcy and Bingley's sisters, is stopped
and Elizabeth is nearly abducted. Darcy steps in
and declares that he and Elizabeth are married.

☐ Hamilton, Maria
Mr. Darcy and the Secret of Becoming a Gentleman
Sourcebooks Landmark, 2011
Darcy feels shy and awkward after Elizabeth
refuses his marriage proposal. He decides to try to
change, which ends up leading him on a journey of
understanding and love.

☐ Harding, PM
Beloved
Meryton Press, 2010
As a newborn, Elizabeth was taken to Staffordshire
and raised in a wealthy family who knew the
Darcys.

☐ Hassell, Ann
Pride and Prejudice's Vampires
Netherfield House Press, 2010
A vampire adaptation of *Pride and Prejudice*.

☐ Head, Gail
An Unforgiving Temper
Alpha Connections, 2011
What if Elizabeth hadn't gone to Pemberley and
what if the events in Ramsgate had ended with
an explosive conflict that set a course filled with
resentment and a thirst for revenge?

☐ Helm, Robin
Guardian
The Guardian Trilogy
Xander Publications, 2011
Xander/Darcy is chief of all guardian angels and
has protected exceptional humans for ten millennia
without losing a battle. Then he receives an
assignment to guard Elizabeth Bennet.

☐ Helm, Robin
SoulFire
The Guardian Trilogy
Robin M. Helm, 2011
A follow-up to *Guardian*.

☐ Helm, Robin M.
Legacy
The Guardian Trilogy (Volume 3)
CreateSpace, 2012
A follow up to *SoulFire* and the final book in this
Christian fantasy trilogy.

☐ Herendeen, Ann
*Pride/Prejudice: A Novel of Mr. Darcy, Elizabeth Bennet,
and Their Forbidden Lovers*
Harper Paperbacks, 2010
Pride/Prejudice focuses on the untold aspects of
Pride and Prejudice including secrets, scandals and
forbidden loves.

☐ Hox, Emma
Longbourn's Unexpected Matchmaker
Rhemalda Publishing, 2010
A retelling that asks what if Colonel Fitzwilliam had been with Bingley and Darcy at Netherfield and who is the mysterious Meryton resident close to the Bennets?

☐ Hoyt, Sarah A. and Skapski, Sofie
A Touch of Night
Naked Reader Press, 2010
A fantasy retelling of *Pride and Prejudice* set in a faraway kingdom.

☐ JB, Edward
Darcy's Dialogues
Lulu.com, 2008
A retelling of *Pride and Prejudice* from Darcy's perspective.

☐ Jeffers, Regina
Darcy's Passions
Ulysses Press, 2009
A retelling of *Pride and Prejudice* from Darcy's perspective.

☑ Jeffers, Regina
Vampire Darcy's Desire
Ulysses Press, 2009
A vampire adaptation of *Pride and Prejudice*.

☐ Kelley, Nancy
His Good Opinion
Smokey Rose Press, 2011
A retelling of *Pride and Prejudice* from Darcy's perspective.

☐ Koehler, Clytie
Lizzy's Choice
CreateSpace, 2011
What if Elizabeth had married Mr. Collins?

☐ Lilian, Lory
Rainy Days
Meryton Press, 2009
Two days after the Netherfield Ball, Darcy and Elizabeth are caught in a rainstorm and forced to spend time alone together talking, listening and getting to know each other.

☐ Lilian, Lory
Remembrance of the Past
Meryton Press, 2009
Rather than running into each other at Pemberley, Darcy and Elizabeth see each other in London.

☐ Listorti, Sandra
Lizzy, the Witch and the Wardrobe: A Sardines Epic
Lulu.com, 2007
A parody in which Lizzy plays a game of sardines with the Bingleys and Mr. Darcy then hides in Miss Bingley's wardrobe and enters a strange world.

☐ Louise, Kara
Master under Good Regulation
Lulu.com, 2010
This book is a retelling of *Pride and Prejudice* from the perspective of Darcy's dog.

☐ Louise, Kara
Darcy's Voyage: A Tale of Uncharted Love on the Open Seas (also published as *Pemberley's Promise*)
Sourcebooks Landmark, 2010
Elizabeth and Darcy, who are travelling separately to America on a ship called Pemberley's Promise, meet and get close after Elizabeth becomes ill and Darcy comes up with a solution to aid in her healing.

☐ Louise, Kara
Assumed Engagement
Lulu.com, 2010
As Darcy is returning to Pemberley from Rosings after his proposal has been refused by Elizabeth, a carriage accident leaves him unconscious. Georgiana, thinking Darcy and Elizabeth are engaged, writes to Elizabeth asking her to come to Pemberley to help Darcy regain consciousness.

☐ Louise, Kara
Only Mr. Darcy Will Do (also published as *Something like Regret*)
Sourcebooks Landmark, 2011
After her father's death, Elizabeth takes a position as a governess working for a family who are acquaintances of the Bingleys and the Darcys.

☐ Mackrory, KaraLynne
Falling for Mr. Darcy
Meryton Press, 2012
When Elizabeth is injured in a fall, Darcy comes to her aid and shows a kinder more charming side to him that makes it easier for her to fall for him.

☐ Mason-Milks, Susan
Mr. Darcy's Proposal
Susan Mason-Milks, 2011
What if Darcy had not proposed to Elizabeth at
Hunsford because she had just received news her
father was ill and not expected to live? Darcy helps
Elizabeth travel home and finds out what she really
thinks of him.

☐ Massey, Beth
Goodly Creatures
CreateSpace, 2012
Darcy and Elizabeth have been linked since
Elizabeth was 15 years old. The story follows their
ups and downs since that time.

☐ McEwen, Gail and Moncton, Tina
Twixt Two Equal Armies
Meryton Press, 2009
Darcy hears that Elizabeth has fled from family
troubles to Scotland and follows under the guise of
a visit to his friend, Lord Baugham.

☐ McEwen, Gail and Moncton, Tina
Love Then Begins
Meryton Press, 2010
A follow-up to *Twixt Two Equal Armies*.

☐ Messick, Gayle Lynn
A World of Expectations, Book 1: The Alliance
CreateSpace, 2010
A retelling of *Pride and Prejudice* from Darcy's
perspective with an added plotline of Darcy's and
Bingley's involvement in a global trading network.

☐ Messick, Gayle Lynn
A World of Expectations, Book 2: The Confrontation
CreateSpace, 2010
A continuation of *World of Expectations, Book 1*.

☐ Miller, Fenella J.
Miss Bennet & Mr. Bingley
Park Publishing, 2009
Pride and Prejudice from Jane's and Charles'
perspectives.

☐ Mushatt, Mary Anne
Darcy and the Duchess
CreateSpace, 2010
Elizabeth meets and marries Rafael Gainsbridge
who dies young. Elizabeth learns to love again with
his best friend, Darcy.

☐ Nattress, Laurel Ann
*Jane Austen Made Me Do It: Original Stories Inspired by
Literature's Most Astute Observer of the Human Heart*
Ballantine Books, 2011
A collection of short stories inspired by Jane
Austen and her works.

☐ Nazarian, Vera
Pride and Platypus: Mr. Darcy's Dreadful Secret
Curiosities, 2012
This otherworldly retelling of *Pride and Prejudice*
features shape-shifting demons and Australian
wildlife mixed with Jane Austen's usual polite
society, satire and romance.

☐ Oaks, Diana J.
One Thread Pulled: The Dance with Mr. Darcy
(Volume 1)
CreateSpace, 2012
Elizabeth does not overhear Darcy's comments at
the Meryton dance and later enters his company
without prejudice.

☐ O'Brien, Sara
Blame it on the Tea
Lulu.com, 2010
When Elizabeth stays at Hunsford rather than going to Rosings she has some tea which changes the outcome of her encounter with Darcy.

☐ O'Brien, Sara
Relations Such as This
Lulu.com, 2009
What if Darcy and Elizabeth met before the Meryton assembly while touring the Netherfield estate and his relations were as questionable as hers?

☐ Odiwe, Jane
Lydia Bennet's Story
Paintbox Publishing, 2007
The story of *Pride and Prejudice* from Lydia's perspective.

☐ Perkins, Charles
Pride and Prejudice on Mars
Unknown, 2010
Pride and Prejudice far removed in time and space.

☐ Pillow, Michelle writing as Annabella Bloom
Pride and Prejudice: The Wild and Wanton Edition
Adams Media, 2011
A "naughty" version of *Pride and Prejudice*.

☐ Reynolds, Abigail
By Force of Instinct
A Pride and Prejudice Variation
Intertidal Press, 2007
Darcy remains at Rosings after his failed proposal and after Elizabeth has read the letter he wrote and they have a chance to get to know each other better.

☐ Reynolds, Abigail
Mr. Fitzwilliam Darcy: The Last Man in the World
A Pride and Prejudice Variation
Sourcebooks, 2010
Elizabeth agrees to marry Darcy after his first proposal and they work through their prejudices to a happy conclusion.

☐ Reynolds, Abigail
To Conquer Mr. Darcy (also published as *Impulse & Initiative*)
A Pride and Prejudice Variation
Sourcebooks Casablanca, 2010
Mr. Darcy doesn't run away after his failed marriage proposal to Elizabeth. Instead he follows her to back to Hertfordshire.

☐ Reynolds, Abigail
Mr. Darcy's Obsession
A Pride and Prejudice Variation
Sourcebooks Landmark, 2010
Elizabeth's father has died forcing the Bennets to leave Longbourn. Darcy finds Elizabeth, but she confuses his marriage proposal as a request to become his mistress.

☐ Reynolds, Abigail
Mr. Darcy's Undoing (also published as *Without Reserve*)
A Pride and Prejudice Variation
Sourcebooks Casablanca, 2011
Elizabeth accepts the proposal of a family acquaintance but Darcy is determined to win her love.

☐ Reynolds, Abigail
What Would Mr. Darcy Do? (also published as *From Lambton to Longbourn*)
A Pride and Prejudice Variation
Sourcebooks Landmark, 2011
What would have happened if Elizabeth and Darcy had spoken of their true feelings after learning Lydia has run off with Wickham rather than assuming the worst about each other?

☐ Reynolds, Abigail
Mr. Darcy's Letter
Intertidal Press, 2011
What if Elizabeth hadn't read the letter Darcy wrote and, unaware of Wickham's nature, revealed all to Wickham putting Darcy and Elizabeth in danger from Wickham's schemes?

☐ Reynolds, Abigail
A Pemberley Medley
A Pride and Prejudice Variation
Interdial Press, 2011
A collection of *Pride and Prejudice* "what if" stories.

☐ Reynolds, Abigail
Mr. Darcy's Refuge
A Pride and Prejudice Variation
White Soup Press, 2012
Darcy and Elizabeth are trapped at the Hunsford Parsonage by a flood just as she has refused his offer of marriage.

☐ Rikard, John A.
Lydia's Lives
CreateSpace, 2011
This book explores how Lydia was driven by a passion that didn't end with Wickham.

☐ Robson, Lynne
Surprises at Rosings
CreateSpace, 2012
What if Lady Catherine had been a nice,
grandmotherly person? Elizabeth enjoys her visit
with Charlotte at Hunsford.

☐ Robson, Lynne
The Journals of Thomas Bennet
CreateSpace, 2011
The journals of Mr. Bennet start when Elizabeth
is born, go through the events of *Pride and Prejudice*
and continue on.

☐ Robson, Lynne
What Until…
CreateSpace, 2012
Elizabeth is distraught over the idea of Jane
eloping. Darcy offers his help.

☐ Sanchez, Laura
A Noteworthy Courtship
CreateSpace, 2009
What if Darcy and the Bingleys had not left
Hertfordshire after the Netherfield Ball?

☐ Saucier, Colette L.
Pulse and Prejudice
Secret Cravings Publishing, 2012
Mr. Darcy meets Elizabeth Bennet and has trouble
controlling his passion for her. He introduces her
to the dark side of London and a world of passion
and the paranormal.

☐ Schamberger, DeDe
Mr. Darcy's Mistake
CreateSpace, 2012
Darcy compromises the woman he loves so she is taken away to protect her reputation. Will the circumstances that divide them bring them together?

☐ Schertz, Melanie A.
A Stitch of Life
CreateSpace, 2012
Elizabeth and her father are in an accident. Mr. Bennet dies but whether or not Elizabeth did becomes unclear when a young woman is discovered who has no memory of who she is.

☐ Schertz, Melanie A.
Governing His Heart
CreateSpace, 2012
Mr. Bennet has died and Elizabeth is taken on as governess to Georgiana Darcy. Will love develop between Elizabeth and Georgiana's brother, Fitzwilliam?

☐ Schertz, Melanie A.
A Pair of Dancing Brown Eyes
CreateSpace, 2012
What if Mr. Bennet's first wife was the mother of Elizabeth and Jane? When she dies and Mr. Bennet remarries, the two girls are sent to live in Lambton near Pemberley.

☐ Schertz, Melanie A.
Storm Clouds of Love
CreateSpace, 2012
After Elizabeth reads Darcy's letter, she is caught in a storm and can't get back to Hunsford Parish. Will Darcy find her and save her?

☐ Schertz, Melanie A.
If Only in His Dreams
CreateSpace, 2012
When Darcy sees Elizabeth at the Meryton dance he knows he wants her for his wife. Does she feel the same? This book also features Darcy's mother and the oldest Bennet child, a son.

☐ Schertz, Melanie A.
With Pen in Hand
CreateSpace, 2012
Elizabeth Bennet has been successful as an author using a man's nom de plume. Now can she find success in a relationship?

☐ Shapiro, Juliette
Fitzwilliam Darcy's Memoirs: An Insight into Jane Austen's Hero
Egerton House Publishing, 2004
Pride and Prejudice from Darcy's perspective.

☐ Silver, Lelia M.
An Unexpected Lady
CreateSpace, 2012
Kitty Bennet is in Kent when she meets an arrogant man who insults her. She tries to avoid him but fails and when they are caught in an embrace, they are forced to marry. Will their feelings for each other grow?

☐ Simonsen, Mary Lydon
For All the Wrong Reasons
CreateSpace, 2011
Darcy realizes he must marry and have a son to be the heir of Pemberley. If Elizabeth marries him she will be in a loveless marriage, but will she do so anyway?

☐ Simonsen, Mary Lydon
A Wife for Mr. Darcy
Sourcebooks Landmark, 2011
Darcy tries to apologize to Elizabeth after insulting
her at the Meryton Assembly but Elizabeth
stands up for herself instead of just accepting his
apology. This intrigues Darcy, but he is already in a
courtship. He has to choose between following his
heart and keeping his honor.

☐ Simonsen, Mary Lydon
A Walk in the Meadows at Rosings Park
Quail Creek Publishing, 2011
Darcy leaves Hertfordshire after the Meryton
assembly believing he's leaving nothing interesting
behind. Then Elizabeth arrives in Kent and he
falls in love with her, but she has not forgotten his
words at the assembly.

☐ Simonsen, Mary Lydon
Darcy and Elizabeth: The Language of the Fan
Quail Creek Publishing, 2011
While Jane recuperates at Netherfield, Elizabeth
and Darcy, frequently together, find their initial
impressions of each other are changing especially
when Elizabeth overhears a conversation between
Darcy and Charles using the language of the fan.

☐ Simonsen, Mary Lydon
Perfect Bride for Mr. Darcy
Sourcebooks Landmark, 2011
Darcy is in a foul mood when he arrives at
Netherfield which accounts for his comments
about Elizabeth. When they meet again at Rosings,
Darcy is attracted to Elizabeth but she still holds a
grudge. Darcy gets help from Anne and Georgiana
in winning Elizabeth over.

☐ Simonsen, Mary Lydon
Mr. Darcy's Bite
Sourcebooks Landmark, 2011
A werewolf-inspired version of *Pride and Prejudice.*

☑ Slater, Maya
The Private Diary of Mr. Darcy (also published as *Mr. Darcy's Diary*)
W.W. Norton, 2009
A retelling of *Pride and Prejudice* from Mr. Darcy's perspective.

☐ Sotis, Wendi
Promises
CreateSpace, 2011
Elizabeth and Darcy have known each other since they were children and over the years their feelings for each other have grown. Will circumstances and interfering family keep them apart?

☐ Sotis, Wendi
Dreams and Expectations
CreateSpace, 2012
Darcy and Elizabeth meet and become friends but misunderstandings may get in the way of deeper feelings developing.

☐ Sotis, Wendi
All Hallow's Eve
CreateSpace, 2012
Elizabeth is High Priestess and leader of an ancient cult and discovers that Darcy, the man she despises, is her Soul Mate.

☑ Street, Mary
The Confession of Fitzwilliam Darcy
Berkley Trade, 2008
A retelling of *Pride and Prejudice* from Darcy's perspective.

☐ Szereto, Mitzi
Pride and Prejudice: Hidden Lusts
Cleis Press, 2011
A retelling of *Pride and Prejudice* focused on each character's desires.

☑ Thwackery, William Codpiece
Fifty Shades of Mr. Darcy
Michael O'Mara, 2012
A mash up *Fifty Shades of Grey* and *Pride and Prejudice* in which Elizabeth is drawn into Darcy's lusty secret world.

☐ Warren, Kate
Wickham's Treachery
Lulu.com, 2007
Details the events when Wickham and Lydia ran off together.

☐ Wasylowski, Karen
Darcy and Fitzwilliam: A Tale of a Gentleman and an Officer
Sourcebooks Landmark, 2011
Darcy's cousin, Richard, has no intention of settling down until he meets American widow Amanda Penrod.

☐ Wasylowski, Karen
Georgiana's Story: Darcy and Fitzwilliam
Sourcebooks Landmark, 2011
Georgiana experiences her first season in London society determined not to disappoint her brother or cousin. Then she meets someone who could change everything.

☐ Webb, Brenda J.
Fitzwilliam Darcy: An Honourable Man
CreateSpace, 2011
Darcy leaves England after Elizabeth refuses his
first proposal. After two years he returns home
thinking he's over Elizabeth. Elizabeth has had a
disastrous marriage. Will Darcy rescue her?

☐ Webb, Brenda J.
Mr. Darcy's Forbidden Love
CreateSpace, 2012
Darcy has been forced into a loveless marriage to
hide his father's sins. Then he meets Elizabeth. Can
they be together?

☐ Wegner, Ola
Moonlighting
CreateSpace, 2009
A retelling in which Darcy is a werewolf and
Elizabeth joins his pack.

☐ Wegner, Ola
Apprehension and Desire
CreateSpace, 2010
What if Elizabeth had agreed to Darcy's first
marriage proposal thinking it was the right thing to
do? Can she fall in love with Darcy?

☐ Wegner, Ola
Deception
CreateSpace, 2010
After the Netherfield ball, Elizabeth meets another
man who is wealthy and attractive. When Darcy and
Elizabeth later meet in Kent how does Darcy deal
with this rival?

☐ Wegner, Ola
The Only Way
CreateSpace, 2011
The day Darcy proposes at Hunsford, Elizabeth hears of her father's death. Will she now consider Darcy's offer?

☐ Wegner, Ola
The Final Reason
CreateSpace, 2012
Elizabeth is engaged when she meets her older brother's friend, Fitzwilliam Darcy.

☐ Wells, Linda
Chance Encounters
CreateSpace, 2008
Darcy and Elizabeth first meet in London and no insults are traded.

☐ Wells, Linda
Fate and Consequences
CreateSpace, 2009
Darcy saves Georgiana from marrying Wickham but the news gets out and Georgiana's reputation is in tatters while Darcy is a humbled man.

☐ Wells, Linda
Memory: Volume 1, Lasting Impressions
CreateSpace, 2010
What if Elizabeth had met Darcy when she was 15 years old and not yet concerned with his potential as a husband?

☐ Wells, Linda
Memory: Volume 2, Trials to Bear
CreateSpace, 2010
A follow-up to *Lasting Impressions*, this book follows the newly wed Elizabeth and Darcy as they move beyond courtship.

☐ Wells, Linda
Memory: Volume 3, How Far We Have Come
CreateSpace, 2010
A follow-up to *Trials to Bear*, the Darcys have a
family of their own and are comfortable with their
positions as the master and mistress of Pemberley.

☐ Whelchel, Lewis
Rocks in the Stream
Meryton Press, 2011
Mr. Bennet has died and Jane is managing
Longbourn. While traveling to Netherfield, Bingley
and Darcy, encounter an injured, unconscious
young woman. While trying to discover her identity
and reunite her with her family, the men learn what
it is to love.

☐ Whelchel, Lewis
Dearly Beloved
Meryton Press, 2012
What if Jane had died from the cold she contract-
ed while riding to Netherfield in the rain?

☐ Wilson, Enid
Bargain with the Devil
Steamy D Publishing, 2009
Darcy helps Lydia but exacts a reward from
Elizabeth for his help.

☐ Wilson, Enid
Really Angelic
Steamy D Publishing, 2009
What angels inhabited England? A paranormal
retelling of Darcy's and Elizabeth's romance.

☐ Wilson, Enid
Fire and Cross
Steamy D Publishing, 2010
A lethal blaze and a garnet cross have ensured that
Darcy's future is promised to an unknown lady.
With danger looming, a suspected spy and a murder
close at hand, will Darcy cross paths with Elizabeth
and win her affection?

☐ Wilson, Enid
Mr. Darcy Mutates…
Steamy D Publishing, 2010
A collection of short stories across the historical,
fantasy and modern genres.

☐ Wilson, Enid
Every Savage Can Reproduce
Steamy D Publishing, 2011
A science fiction version of Pride and Prejudice
set in the 39th century. Elizabeth is accused of
luring Darcy to an illegal establishment, which leads
to their exile on a rebel planet and a subsequent
galactic war.

☐ Wilson, Enid
Mr. Darcy Vibrates…
Steamy D Publishing, 2011
A collection of short stories across the historical,
fantasy and modern genres.

☐ Wilson, Enid
*The Spinster's Vow: A Spicy Retelling of Mrs. Darcy's
Journey to Love*
CreateSpace, 2011
Mr. Bennet goes missing and the Bennet women
leave Longbourn. Mr. Darcy meets sad but spirited
Elizabeth who is determined to find her father
before anything else.

☐ Wilson, Enid, Avery, Aimee and Williams, June
Honor and Integrity
CreateSpace, 2012
A collection of nine short stories inspired by *Pride and Prejudice*.

☐ Woodbury, Katherine
A Man of Few Words
Peaks Island Press, 2011
Darcy offers his perspective on his relationship with Elizabeth Bennet.

SEQUELS

☐ Adams, Aimee E.
Affairs of the Heart: The First Twelve Years
Ada S. Robarge, 2012
A sequel covering the twelve years following Elizabeth's and Darcy's wedding.

☐ Adkins, Samantha
Expectations
CreateSpace, 2010
A sequel commencing six months after the Darcys' wedding. Appearances by Georgiana Darcy and Lydia Wickham.

☐ Aiken, Joan
Lady Catherine's Necklace
Indigo Paperbacks, 2001
This sequel centers on Lady Catherine de Bourgh and others at Rosings Park.

☐ Aitken, Virginia
Mary Bennet's Chance
Pen Press Publishers, 2011
The story of Mary Bennet three years after the conclusion of *Pride and Prejudice*.

Altman, Marsha
The Darcys & the Bingleys: A Tale of Two Gentlemen's Marriages to Two Most Devoted Sisters
Pride & Prejudice Continues
Sourcebooks Landmark, 2008
Covers preparations for the wedding night, Darcy's and Bingley's friendship, Caroline Bingley and Georgiana Darcy.

Altman, Marsha
The Plight of the Darcy Brothers: A Tale of Siblings and Surprises
Pride & Prejudice Continues
Sourcebooks Landmark, 2009
Follow-up to *The Darcys & the Bingleys* taking place years later and focusing on the children of the two couples, Mary Bennet and the return of Wickham.

Altman, Marsha
Mr. Darcy's Great Escape: A Tale of the Darcys & the Bingleys
Pride & Prejudice Continues
Sourcebooks Landmark, 2010
Follow-up to *The Plight of the Darcy Brothers*, this installment takes place in 1812 with the backdrop of the Napoleonic Wars.

Altman, Marsha
The Ballad of Gregoire Darcy
Pride & Prejudice Continues
Ulysses Press, 2011
Fourth in the series, this book focuses on Mr. Darcy's illegitimate brother Gregoire, Mr. Bennet's advancing years and the courtship of Mary Bennet.

☐ Altman, Marsha
The Road to Pemberley: An Anthology of New Pride and Prejudice Stories
Pride & Prejudice Continues
Ulysses Press, 2011
A collection of short stories by Regency romance authors that feature Jane Austen characters.

☐ Altman, Marsha
Knights of Derbyshire
Pride & Prejudice Continues
Laughing Man Productions, 2012
Fifth in the series, this book takes place twenty years after Elizabeth and Darcy married. All of the Bennet sisters are settled but trouble lurks and the political situation in Georgian England affects their lives.

☐ Altman, Marsha
Georgiana and the Wolf
Pride & Prejudice Continues
CreateSpace, 2012
Sixth in the series, this book is focused on a mystery involving Georgiana Bingley who is the daughter of Charles and Jane Bingley.

☐ Aminadra, Karen
Charlotte ~ Pride and Prejudice Continues
Unknown , 2012
As Charlotte becomes part of Hunsford society she realizes how many others have been hurt by Lady Catherine. She must decide whether to keep quiet or try and make changes.

☐ Aston, Elizabeth
Mr. Darcy's Daughters
Touchstone, 2003
Elizabeth and Darcy go on a diplomatic mission leaving their five daughters in London with Colonel Fitzwilliam and his wife.

☐ Aston, Elizabeth
The Exploits & Adventures of Miss Alethea Darcy
Orion Publishing, 2004
Elizabeth's and Darcy's youngest daughter who, after entering a regrettable marriage, takes steps to escape.

☐ Aston, Elizabeth
The True Darcy Spirit
Touchstone, 2006
Cassandra Darcy, the daughter of Anne de Bourgh, is an artist struggling to support herself in London.

☐ Aston, Elizabeth
The Second Mrs. Darcy
Touchstone, 2007
Continuation of the Darcy family saga, this time focused on Octavia Darcy, widow of Darcy's cousin Christopher.

☐ Aston, Elizabeth
The Darcy Connection
Touchstone, 2008
The daughters of Mr. Collins try to make advantageous marriages.

☐ Aston, Elizabeth
Mr. Darcy's Dream
Touchstone, 2009
Phoebe, Mr. Darcy's young niece, has retreated to Pemberley after an unhappy romance. She is joined by the also single Louisa Bingley and the two meet handsome strangers and prepare for a ball.

☐ Ayers, John D.
Mr. Darcy Parries Forth in Love (Volume 1)
CreateSpace, 2012
A *Pride and Prejudice* sequel that follows Elizabeth and Darcy from six weeks after their wedding.

☐ Bader, Ted and Bader, Marilyn
Desire and Duty
Revive, 1997
A sequel to *Pride and Prejudice* that focuses on
Georgiana Darcy.

☐ Bader, Ted and Bader, Marilyn
Virtue and Vanity
Revive, 2000
A follow-up to *Desire and Duty* that features Sarah
Bingley as governess for Georgiana's children and
follows her relationship with Andrew Darcy, heir of
Pemberley.

☐ Baker, Helen
Book of Ruth
Helen Baker, 2011
This sequel takes place at Longbourn five years
after the conclusion of *Pride and Prejudice* and
follows the stories of Kitty and Mary who still live
there, unwed and unhappy.

☐ Barrett, Julia
Presumption
M. Evans And Company, 1993
This sequel continues with the characters of *Pride
and Prejudice* taking on storylines previously held
by other characters – Georgiana has an Elizabeth
storyline, Caroline acts like Lydia, etc.

☐ Barrington, E. (aka Lily Adams Beck)
The Ladies! A Shining Constellation of Wit and Beauty
Unknown, 1922
A collection of short stories, one of which is called
"The Darcys of Rosings Park." It takes place when
the eldest Darcy child is seventeen and Elizabeth
and Darcy have inherited Rosings. Also included are
the Wickhams and Marianne and Willoughby.

☑ Bebris, Carrie
Pride and Prescience (Or, a *Truth Universally Acknowledged*)
Mr. and Mrs. Darcy Mystery
Forge Books, 2004
A mystery with Elizabeth and Darcy as sleuths.

☑ Bebris, Carrie
Suspense and Sensibility (Or, First Impressions Revisited)
Mr. and Mrs. Darcy Mystery
Forge Books, 2005
A mystery with Elizabeth and Darcy as sleuths.

☑ Bebris, Carrie
North by Northanger (Or, the *Shades of Pemberley*)
Mr. and Mrs. Darcy Mystery
Forge Books, 2007
A mystery with Elizabeth and Darcy as sleuths.

☑ Bebris, Carrie
Matters at Mansfield (Or, the *Crawford Affair*)
Mr. and Mrs. Darcy Mystery
Forge Books, 2008
A mystery with Elizabeth and Darcy as sleuths.

☑ Bebris, Carrie
The Intrigue at Highbury (Or, *Emma's Match*)
Mr. and Mrs. Darcy Mystery
Tor Books, 2010
A mystery with Elizabeth and Darcy as sleuths.

☑ Bebris, Carrie
The Deception at Lyme (Or, *The Peril of Persuasion*)
Mr. and Mrs. Darcy Mystery
Tor Books, 2011
A mystery with Elizabeth and Darcy as sleuths.

☐ Becton, Jennifer
Charlotte Collins
Whitely Press, 2010
This sequel focuses on Charlotte Collins' life up to and after the death of Mr. Collins.

☐ Becton, Jennifer
Caroline Bingley: A Continuation of Jane Austen's Pride and Prejudice
Whitely Press, 2011
A sequel focusing on Caroline Bingley and her refusal to make amends with Elizabeth.

☐ Becton, Jennifer
Maria Lucas (also published as *Maria's Romance*)
Whitely Press, 2011
A short story focusing on Maria Lucas.

☑ Berdoll, Linda
Mr. Darcy Takes a Wife (also published as *The Bar Sinister*)
Sourcebooks Landmark, 2004
A sequel that picks up at the beginning of the Victorian age.

☑ Berdoll, Linda
Darcy & Elizabeth: Nights and Days at Pemberley
Sourcebooks Landmark, 2006
A follow-up to *Darcy Takes a Wife*.

☐ Berdoll, Linda
The Darcys: Ruling Passion
Well There It Is, 2011
A follow-up to *Darcy & Elizabeth*.

☐ Birchall, Diana
Mrs. Darcy's Dilemma
Sourcebooks Landmark, 2008
A sequel that picks up at the beginning of the Victorian age.

☐ Bonavia-Hunt, D.A.
Pemberley Shades
E.P. Dutton, 1949
This book picks up several years after the end of
Pride and Prejudice and is "lightly gothic."

☑ Brinton, Sybil G.
*Old Friends and New Fancies: An Imaginary Sequel to the
Novels of Jane Austen*
Unknown, 1913
Considered the first Jane Austen fan-fiction story
conceived, the author takes characters from all
of Jane Austen's novels and weaves them into a
"concluding" story.

☐ Brocklehurst, Judith
Darcy and Anne (also published as *A Letter from Lady
Catherine*)
Sourcebooks Landmark; 2009
This sequel focuses on Anne de Bourgh and her
improvement when separated from her mother.

☐ Burnett, Jean
The Bad Miss Bennet
Pegasus, 2012
A sequel focused on Lydia who at twenty is a
widow and in search of a new husband.

☐ Burris, Skylar Hamilton
Conviction
Double Edge Press, 2006
This book continues the story of *Pride and Prejudice*
focusing on Georgiana Darcy and her suitors.

☐ Burris, Skylar Hamilton
An Unlikely Missionary
Double Edge Press, 2008
A sequel to *Pride and Prejudice* that focuses on
Charlotte Collins.

☐ Burris, Skylar Hamilton
The Strange Marriage of Anne de Bourgh
Ancient Paths Publications, 2010
A sequel to *Pride and Prejudice* that focuses on Anne de Bourgh.

☐ Caldwell, Jack
The Three Colonels: Jane Austen's Fighting Men
Sourcebooks Landmark, 2012
Bringing together two stories, Colonels Fitzwilliam, Buford (fiance of Caroline Bingley) and Brandon lead peaceful lives until the escape of Napoleon from exile.

☐ CI, Victoria
A More Prosperous Trial of the State
Lulu.com, 2007
This sequel picks up a couple of months after Elizabeth's and Darcy's wedding and focuses on Caroline Bingley and her suitors. It also brings in characters from *Mansfield Park*.

☑ Collins, Rebecca Ann
The Pemberley Chronicles
The Pemberley Chronicles
Sourcebooks Landmark, 2008
This sequel starts after the wedding of Darcy and Elizabeth.

☑ Collins, Rebecca Ann
The Women of Pemberley
The Pemberley Chronicles
Sourcebooks Landmark, 2008
This sequel follows the lives of various women, some from Jane Austen's novels, as they enter the Victorian era in post-industrial England.

☐ Collins, Rebecca Ann
Netherfield Park Revisited
The Pemberley Chronicles
Sourcebooks Landmark, 2008
This sequel takes place during mid-Victorian England and focuses on the son of Jane and Charles, Jonathan Bingley, after he purchases Netherfield Park.

☐ Collins, Rebecca Ann
The Ladies of Longbourn
The Pemberley Chronicles
Sourcebooks Landmark, 2008
This book is a follow-up to *Netherfield Park Revisited* and centers on the wife and daughter of Jonathan Bingley (who is now the owner of Longbourn), and Charlotte Collins.

☐ Collins, Rebecca Ann
Mr. Darcy's Daughter
The Pemberley Chronicles
Sourcebooks Landmark, 2008
This book tells the story of Cassy Darcy, daughter of Darcy and Elizabeth, who is married and the mother of five. She faces a challenge when her brother Julian has trouble as heir to the Pemberley estate.

☐ Collins, Rebecca Ann
My Cousin Caroline
The Pemberley Chronicles
Sourcebooks Landmark, 2009
This sequel focuses on Colonel Fitzwilliam and Caroline Gardiner, the daughter of Mr. and Mrs. Gardiner.

☐ Collins, Rebecca Ann
Postscript from Pemberley
The Pemberley Chronicles
Sourcebooks Landmark, 2009
This book follows the characters developed in
the author's previous works – Julian Darcy, Jessica
Courtney and Darcy Gardiner – and a newcomer to
Pemberley, Kate O'Hare.

☐ Collins, Rebecca Ann
Recollections of Rosings
The Pemberley Chronicles
Sourcebooks Landmark, 2010
This sequel is focused on the daughters of
Charlotte Lucas and Mr. Collins, Becky Tate and
Catherine Harrison.

☐ Collins, Rebecca Ann
A Woman of Influence
The Pemberley Chronicles
Sourcebooks Landmark, 2010
This book follows up *Recollections of Rosings* with
more on Becky Tate.

☐ Collins, Rebecca Ann
The Legacy of Pemberley
The Pemberley Chronicles
Sourcebooks Landmark, 2010
This book closes out the author's series and weaves
together the characters and themes from previous
novels.

☐ Creek, Amethyst
The Next Generation
Unknown, 2012
This sequel focuses on the daughters of the Darcys,
the Wickhams and the Collinses.

☑ Dawkins, Jane
Letters from Pemberley: The First Year
Sourcebooks Landmark, 2007
Letters from Elizabeth Darcy to her sister Jane describe her first year of marriage.

☑ Dawkins, Jane
More Letters from Pemberley
Sourcebooks Landmark, 2007
A follow-up to *Letters from Pemberley* that picks up at the end of that book and includes letters from Elizabeth covering the next six years.

☐ de Jong, Cornelis
My Brother and I
C.A. de Jong, 2010
A sequel from the point of view a young man of no consequence, looking in from the outside but becoming drawn into the world at Pemberley.

☐ Delman, Joan Ellen
Miss de Bourgh's Adventure
Lulu.com, 2005
This continuation focuses on Lady Catherine's resolve to find Anne a husband.

☐ Elliott, Anna
Georgiana Darcy's Diary
Pride and Prejudice Chronicles
Anna Elliott, 2011
A sequel focusing on Georgiana Darcy and her suitors.

☐ Elliott, Anna
Pemberley to Waterloo: Georgiana Darcy's Diary, Volume 2
Pride and Prejudice Chronicles
Wilton Press, 2011
A follow-up to *Georgiana Darcy's Diary*.

☐ Fafoutakis, Anne
Mrs. Fitzwilliam Darcy and Other Stories
Upfront Publishing, 2002
A collection of short stories including one that
features the Darcys' life after marriage.

☐ Fairview, Monica
The Other Mr. Darcy: Did You Know Mr. Darcy Had an American Cousin?
Sourcebooks Landmark, 2009
A sequel featuring Caroline Bingley and Darcy's
American cousin, Robert.

☐ Fairview, Monica
The Darcy Cousins
Sourcebooks Landmark, 2010
A sequel focusing on Georgiana Darcy and Darcy's
American cousin, Clarissa.

☐ Farmer, Ava
Second Impressions
Chawton House Press, 2011
A sequel that spans 10 years after the end of *Pride and Prejudice*.

☐ Frederic, Mariette
Pride and Prejudice Surrendered
Rosedog Press, 2010
A sequel that focuses on the question of whether
Elizabeth or Darcy became estranged from their
respective families.

☐ Furley, Phyllis
The Darcys: Scenes from Married Life
Egerton House Publishing, 2004
This sequel spans the first two years of the Darcys'
marriage and is focused on Mr. Darcy.

☐ Gatje-Smith, Norma
The Sequel to Jane Austen's Pride and Prejudice: Trust and Triumph
AuthorHouse, 2004
This sequel chronicles the lives of the Darcys, Bingleys and Bennets.

☐ Geare, Michael and Geare, David Holloway
Nothing So Became Them: Some Improved Obituaries
Buchan & Enright, 1986
This book offers a number of fictional obituaries including one for Mr. Collins.

☐ Gillespie, Jane
Teverton Hall
St. Martin's Press, 1987
This sequel takes place 20 years after the end of the novel and focuses on the Collinses and their children.

☐ Gillespie, Jane
Deborah
Robert Hale, 1995
This sequel focuses on Anne de Bourgh.

☐ Grange, Amanda and Webb, Jacqueline
Pride and Pyramids: Mr. Darcy in Egypt
Sourcebooks, 2012
The Darcys travel to Egypt where they uncover a mystery involving an ancient Egyptian woman.

☐ Grange, Amanda, Lathan, Sharon and Eberhart, Carolyn
A Darcy Christmas
Sourcebooks Landmark, 2010
Three short stories centering on Elizabeth and Darcy at Christmas time.

☑ Grange, Amanda
Mr. Darcy, Vampyre
Sourcebooks Landmark, 2009
A sequel in which Darcy reveals himself to be a
vampire.

☐ Halstead, Helen
Mr. Darcy Presents His Bride (also published as *Private
Performance*)
Ulysses Press, 2007
This book continues the *Pride and Prejudice* story and
describes Elizabeth's life in London society.

☐ Hampson, Anne
Pemberley Place
Dales Large Print, 1998
In this sequel, Mr. Collins dies leaving Charlotte
available to remarry and Mr. Bennet becomes sole
owner of Longbourn as the entail is broken.

☐ Hanson, Barrie
Love & Duty
Lulu.com, 2007
A sequel that follows the lives of Mary and Kitty
Bennet and Anne de Bourgh.

☐ Hensley, Cynthia Ingram
Echoes of Pemberley
Meryton Press, 2011
A plane crash has left Catherine Elizabeth Darcy an
orphan in the care of her brother, Bennet.

☑ Hockensmith, Steve
Pride and Prejudice and Zombies: Dreadfully Ever After
Quirk Books, 2011
A sequel and conclusion to *Pride and Prejudice and
Zombies*.

☐ Hogstrom, Marie
Derbyshire
BookSurge Publishing, 2008
A sequel that has Elizabeth acting and judging on
her own since she is no longer as close to Jane.

☑ James, PD
Death Comes to Pemberley
Faber and Faber, 2011
After six years of marriage, life is good for Darcy
and Elizabeth until Lydia arrives shrieking that
Wickham has been murdered.

☐ JB, Edward
Pemberley Pen Pals
Lulu.com, 2008
Elizabeth and Jane write letters to each other while
awaiting the births of their children.

☐ Jeffers, Regina
Darcy's Dreams
Xlibris, 2008
This sequel to *Pride and Prejudice* picks up four
months into Darcy's and Elizabeth's marriage.

☐ Jeffers, Regina
Darcy's Temptation
Ulysses Press, 2009
A sequel to *Pride and Prejudice* that starts four
months after the wedding with Elizabeth pregnant
and Darcy tempted by another woman.

☐ Jeffers, Regina
The Phantom of Pemberley
Ulysses Press, 2010
After a snowstorm strands a group of travelers
at Pemberley, accidents and deaths occur that
are attributed to a phantom that has haunted
Pemberley. Darcy and Elizabeth, however, think
someone is trying to murder them.

☐ Jeffers, Regina
Christmas at Pemberley
Ulysses Press, 2011
The Bennets and the Bingleys are invited to
Christmas at Pemberley. En route to the estate,
Darcy and Elizabeth are stalled by a blizzard at an
inn. At Pemberley, Georgiana Darcy tries to manage
the chaos of the guests who have arrived.

☐ Jeffers, Regina
The Disappearance of Georgiana Darcy
A Pride and Prejudice Mystery
Ulysses Press, 2012
After leaving home in Scotland to be reunited
with her husband, Georgiana disappears then is
presumed dead. Darcy and Elizabeth travel to
Scotland to search for her and try to solve the
mystery of what happened to her.

☐ Jeffers, Regina
The Mysterious Death of Mr. Darcy
A Pride and Prejudice Mystery
Ulysses Press, 2013
Following the sudden death of the cousin of
Darcy's father, Elizabeth and Darcy go to Dorset to
pay their respects. While there, strange events occur.

☐ Kaye-Smith, Sheila and Stern, G.B.
More Talk of Jane Austen
Cassell, 1950
This book includes speculation about the lives of
those in Jane Austen's six complete novels.

☐ Kerr, Meg
Experience
Bluebell Publishing, 2011
A sequel that begins when Darcy and Elizabeth
arrive at Pemberley on their honeymoon.

☑ Lathan, Sharon
Mr. and Mrs. Fitzwilliam Darcy: Two Shall Become One
Sourcebooks Landmark, 2009
A continuation spanning the first five months of Darcy's and Elizabeth's marriage. First book in a series.

☑ Lathan, Sharon
Loving Mr. Darcy: Journeys Beyond Pemberley
Sourcebooks Landmark, 2009
A story of Darcy and Elizabeth after their first few months at Pemberley, in London and beyond. The second book in a series.

☐ Lathan, Sharon
My Dearest Mr. Darcy: An Amazing Journey into Love Everlasting
Sourcebooks Landmark, 2010
This book picks up when the Darcys have been married nine months and are awaiting the birth of their first child. It continues through the end of their first year of marriage. The third book in a series.

☐ Lathan, Sharon
In the Arms of Mr. Darcy
Sourcebooks Landmark, 2010
Starting a year after the Darcy's marriage, this book is the fourth book in a series.

☐ Lathan, Sharon
The Trouble with Mr. Darcy
Sourcebooks Landmark, 2011
The fifth installment in series, this book sees the return of George Wickham.

☐ Lathan, Sharon
The Passions of Dr. Darcy
Sourcebooks, 2013
Darcy and Elizabeth's second son is a doctor who travels to India to work then returns to Pemberley after thirty years.

☐ Lathan, Sharon
Miss Darcy Falls in Love
Sourcebooks Landmark, 2011
Georgiana Darcy has two very different men competing to win her heart.

☐ Long, Ian
Better Judgement
Ian Long, 2006
A sequel that picks up four years after the end of the novel.

☐ Louise, Kara
Assumed Obligation
Lulu.com, 2010
This book follows up *Assumed Engagement* and chronicles the Darcys after their marriage with a focus on Georgiana's romance which proceeds in a way similar to that of Elizabeth and Darcy.

☐ Louise, Kara
Pemberley Celebrations - The First Year
Heartwork Publications, 2011
A collection of short stories spanning the Darcys' first year of marriage as they celebrate holidays and special events.

☐ Mackey, Nacie
A Woman Worthy
Lulu.com, 2007
This book is a *Pride and Prejudice* sequel.

☑ McCullough, Colleen
The Independence of Miss Mary Bennet
Simon & Schuster, 2008
This sequel takes place 20 years after the end of
Pride and Prejudice and no one's life has turned
out well. The title refers to Mary setting out to
document England's poor.

☐ Moffat, Isobel Scott
Mistress of Pemberley
Athena Press, 2008
Elizabeth plays matchmaker for Georgiana and
Anne de Bourgh while back at Longbourn, Kitty,
Mary and Mr. Bennet have fallen under the spell of
a Mrs. Castlemain.

☐ Morgan, Frances
Darcy and Elizabeth
Cenfar Books, 2003
This sequel picks up six months after the marriage
of Elizabeth and Darcy and follows a year or so.

☐ Morgan, Frances
Darcy's Pemberley
Cenfar Books, 2004
A continuation of *Darcy and Elizabeth* that covers
the couple through another year.

☐ Nelson, Kathryn L.
Pemberley Manor: Darcy and Elizabeth, for Better or for Worse
Sourcebooks Landmark, 2009
This sequel starts after the wedding of Darcy and
Elizabeth and chronicles several months.

☐ Newark, Elizabeth
Consequence: Or, Whatever Became of Charlotte Lucas
New Ark Productions, 1997
This sequel is focused on Charlotte Lucas and her
marriage to Mr. Collins.

☐ Newark, Elizabeth
The Darcys Give a Ball: A Gentle Joke, Jane Austen Style
Sourcebooks Landmark, 2008
This sequel chronicles the lives of the children of
Jane, Elizabeth and Georgiana who form their own
relationships, sometimes with each other.

☐ Nieves, Doris
Misconceptions
Xlibris, 2010
Mrs. Bennet continues to look for husbands for
Mary and Kitty while Lady Catherine searches for
one for Anne.

☐ Odiwe, Jane
Mr. Darcy's Secret
Sourcebooks Landmark, 2011
A sequel beginning when Elizabeth moves into
Pemberley. She's learning to be mistress of
the estate, trying to reconcile Darcy and Lady
Catherine, helping Georgiana come out of her shell
and dealing with rumors about Darcy's past.

☐ Orlando, Eugene
A Marriage of Reason
Scriptor Publishing Company, 2010
This sequel focuses on Mary Bennet.

☐ Park, Victoria
Pride and Prejudice II: The Sequel
AuthorHouse, 2010
A sequel that spans the time from Darcy's and
Elizabeth's wedding to the late 18th century and
chronicles the lives of those associated with
Pemberley.

☐ Pierson, C. Allyn (aka Carey Bligard)
And This Our Life
Chronicles of the Darcy Family
iUniverse, 2008
This book covers the first year of Elizabeth's and Darcy's marriage.

☐ Pierson, C. Allyn (aka Carey Bligard)
Mr. Darcy's Little Sister
Pride & Prejudice Continues
Sourcebooks Landmark, 2010
This sequel focuses on Georgiana Darcy.

☐ Pinnock, Jonathan
Mrs Darcy versus the Aliens
Salt, 2011
In this sequel, Lydia has been abducted by aliens and Elizabeth may need to work with Wickham to save her. Meanwhile Mr. Collins is running a home for fallen women while Charlotte has become a drug addict.

☐ Russell, Anne and Russell, Arthur
Wedding at Pemberley: A Footnote to Pride and Prejudice, a Play in One Act
Walter H. Baker, 1949
A very brief one-act play that takes place during the preparations for Georgiana's wedding.

☐ Sarath, Patrice
The Unexpected Miss Bennet
Berkley Trade, 2011
A *Pride and Prejudice* sequel focused on Mary Bennet.

☐ Shapiro, Juliette
Mr. Darcy's Decision (also published as *Excessively Diverted*)
Ulysses Press, 2008
This book has the newly wed Darcys beginning their lives together at Pemberley, happily, but soon social enemies undermine their tranquility.

☐ Sherwood, Mary L.
A Marriage Worth the Earning: To Have and to Hold
CreateSpace, 2009
This sequel focuses on the first year of Darcy's and Elizabeth's marriage.

☐ Sherwood, Mary L.
A Marriage Worth the Earning: For Better for Worse
CreateSpace, 2010
This is a continuation of *A Marriage Worth the Earning: To Have and to Hold* and continues to focus on the Darcys' first year of marriage.

☐ Silver, Lelia M.
An Unlikely Duet
CreateSpace, 2012
This sequel focuses on Georgiana Darcy and starts five years after Elizabeth and Darcy marry.

☐ St. Clair, Sophie
Mary King
Unknown, 2011
A graphic novel in several volumes focuses on Mary King.

☐ Strand, Richard S.
Pemberleyman, Volume 1: Obligation & Obsession
CreateSpace, 2012
A *Pride and Prejudice* sequel that exposes secrets and answers questions about the book's characters.

☐ Tennant, Emma
Pemberley
St. Martin's Press, 1993
This sequel starts one year after the wedding of
Elizabeth and Darcy and focuses on a gathering
that includes both their families.

☐ Tennant, Emma
An Unequel Marriage
Sceptre, 1995
This book picks up when the Darcys have been
married for nearly 20 years and includes the
happenings of their two children, a daughter like
Elizabeth and an out of control son.

☐ Unknown
Gambles and Gambols: A Visit with Old Friends
Shelter Cove, 1983
This book is a *Mansfield Park* sequel that focuses
on Edmund's advancement in the church and
Fanny's search for a wife for Tom. Also included
are characters from *Pride and Prejudice*, *Emma* and
Persuasion.

☐ Walkley, Arthur Bingham
Pastiche and Prejudice
Knopf, 1921
Mr. Collins is invited by his brother to a play in
London and Lady Catherine decides to accompany
him and Mrs. Collins. There is disapproval of a
later event that forces Mr. Collins to express Lady
Catherine's and his disapproval.

☐ Walls, Cedric
Heiress of Rosings: A Play in Three Acts
S. French, 1956
A play featuring Anne de Bourgh.

☐ Ward, Eucharista
Illusions and Ignorance: Mary Bennet's Story
Outskirts Press, 2007
This novel revisits the Bennet family a few years after *Pride and Prejudice* concludes. Mary Bennet observes her sisters' marriages and has changing opinions of marriage for herself.

☐ Ward, Eucharista
A Match for Mary Bennet
Sourcebooks Landmark, 2009
After Elizabeth's marriage, Mary is relieved she won't be obliged to marry and that she's free to continue her faithful work.

☐ Wasylowski, Karen V.
Sons and Daughters: Darcy and Fitzwilliam, Book Two
CreateSpace, 2012
The story of Darcy and his cousin Richard and their wives and children.

☐ Wegner, Ola
No Other Way
CreateSpace, 2012
A *Pride and Prejudice* sequel.

☐ Wells, Linda
Imperative, Volume 1
CreateSpace, 2012
A sequel that focuses on Darcy trying to do right by Elizabeth and Georgiana.

☐ Wells, Linda
Imperative, Volume 2
CreateSpace, 2012
A follow-up to *Imperative, Volume 1*.

☐ Wilkin, DW
Colonel Fitzwilliam's Correspondence
Regency Assembly Press, 2011
A sequel to *Pride and Prejudice* focused on Colonel
Fitzwilliam.

☐ Wimer, Genevieve R.
Honour and Humility
Sutter House, 2002
A *Pride and Prejudice* sequel.

☐ Winslow, Shannon
The Darcys of Pemberley
Heather Ridge Arts, 2011
A sequel that picks up when Elizabeth and Darcy
have been married for almost a year. Their idyllic
life at Pemberley is jeopardized by secrets, their
friends' troubles and the threat of a villain in their
midst.

CONTEMPORARY

☐ Anderson, Winter K.
One Good Man or Two
Anderson-Zechman, 2012
A mature adult contemporary take on *Pride and
Prejudice* that features Elizabeth Bennet and her
suitors - William Darcy, Richard Fitzwilliam, Bill
Collins and George Wickham.

☐ Andi, Beverley
Searching for Mr. Darcy
Unknown, 2011
Megan Mills, an English teacher, takes a summer
job with a Scottish writer and falls for him and his
friend. Is one of them her Mr. Darcy?

☐ Angelini, Sara
The Trials of the Honorable F. Darcy
Sourcebooks Landmark, 2009
Darcy is a judge and Elizabeth is an attorney.

☐ Austen, Jan
A Single Man, Good Fortune (Must Want Wife)
American Pride & Prejudice
iUniverse, 2004
An updated version of *Pride and Prejudice* that covers
sexual politics and family relations during the 80s
in New England. This book kicks off a series and
focuses on Mathew and Zola Bennet-Towne.

☐ Austen, Jan
The Arts for Captivation
American Pride & Prejudice
iUniverse, 2005
An updated version of *Pride and Prejudice* that covers
sexual politics and family relations during the 80s
in New England. This second entry in the series
focuses on John Bing and Mary Jane Bennet-
Towne.

☐ Austen, Jan
Pleasures of Youth
American Pride & Prejudice
iUniverse, 2006
An updated version of *Pride and Prejudice* that covers
sexual politics and family relations during the 80s in
New England. This third entry in the series focuses
on the story of Michael Wickham and Lydia
Bennet-Towne.

☐ Austen, Jan
Politics of Sex
American Pride & Prejudice
iUniverse, 2007
An updated version of *Pride and Prejudice* that covers sexual politics and family relations during the 80s in New England. This final book in the series focuses on Nick D'Arcini and Elizabeth Bennet-Towne.

☐ Austen, Jan
American Pride & Prejudice: Great American Novel on the Politics of Sex
iUniverse, 2009
This book includes the four separate entries of the American Pride & Prejudice series.

☐ Avery, Aimee
A Little Bit Psychic: Pride & Prejudice with a Modern Twist
CreateSpace, 2009
Elizabeth Bennet is in London studying for a PhD. She's a little bit psychic and sees her future with Darcy.

☐ Baxley, M.K.
The Cumberland Plateau: A Pride and Prejudice Modern Sequel
CreateSpace, 2009
This contemporary story tells how the Darcys and Bennets have long standing family ties and follows two brothers, descendants of Mr. Darcy.

☐ Baxley, M.K.
Dana Darcy: The Pride and Prejudice Sequel to The Cumberland Plateau
CreateSpace, 2010
This book is a continuation of *The Cumberland Plateau.*

☐ Benneton, Nina
Compulsively Mr. Darcy
Sourcebooks Landmark, 2012
Darcy is a wealthy philanthropist with obsessive
tendencies while Dr. Elizabeth Bennet deals with
intimacy issues. Can the two accept each other?

☐ Bianchi, Moira
*Friendship of a Special Kind: A Novel Inspired by Pride
and Prejudice, Mr. Darcy and His Everlasting Appeal*
(Volume 1)
CreateSpace, 2012
Pride and Prejudice with a sexy, Brazilian touch.
Elizabeth and William meet when they're in their
30s and aren't looking for anything serious until
William falls in love.

☐ Brant, Marilyn
According to Jane
Kensington, 2009
After Ellie Barnett is assigned *Pride and Prejudice*
in high school, Jane Austen becomes her voice
of reason, guiding Ellie through the years and
boyfriends to come.

☐ Briggs, Laura and Burgess, Sarah
Dear Miss Darcy
CreateSpace, 2012
Olivia Darcy is a love columnist and a descendant
of Lizzie and Darcy but neither has guaranteed her
a happy ending in love until an advice letter pits her
wits against those of a notorious bachelor.

☐ Brokow, Andrea Marie
Pride, Prejudice, and Curling Rocks
Hedgie Press, 2011
Darcy Bennet enjoys curling and has an eye for
Lucas Fitzwilliam.

☐ Brown, Mary Calhoun
*Pride & Prejudice with a Side of Grits: A Southern-fried
Version of Jane Austen's Classic*
Wentworth & Collins, 2012
A backwoods, modern adaptation of *Pride and
Prejudice*.

☐ Caldwell, Jack
Pemberley Ranch
Sourcebooks Landmark, 2010
Pride and Prejudice retold as a US Western romance.

☐ Canton, Chamein
Waiting for Mr. Darcy
Genesis Press, 2009
Three boarding school friends looking for their
own Mr. Darcy.

☐ Cohen, Paula Marantz
Jane Austen in Boca
St. Martin's Griffin, 2003
The Bennet daughters are portrayed as elderly
Jewish widows in a Boca retirement community.

☐ Cole, Barbara Tiller
White Lies and Other Half Truths
CreateSpace, 2008
A contemporary version of *Pride and Prejudice*
written as a sexy farce.

☑ Connelly, Victoria
A Weekend with Mr. Darcy
Sourcebooks Landmark, 2011
Professor Katherine Roberts enjoys Jane Austen
and racy Regency romance novels. She attends a
Jane Austen Addicts conference where a handsome
man sweeps her off her feet.

☐ Connelly, Victoria
Dreaming of Mr. Darcy
Sourcebooks Landmark, 2012
Kay Ashton is in Lyme finishing her book, *The Illustrated Mr. Darcy*. A film company working on a new adaptation of *Persuasion* arrives and Kay is taken with the actor playing Captain Wentworth, however the screenwriter Adam Craig may be her Mr. Darcy.

☐ Cooper-Thumann, Rebecca A.
The London Chronicles
CreateSpace, 2010
The story of sisters Olivia and Jane, their cousin, Samantha, and the three men who catch their attention.

☐ Cooper-Thumann, Rebecca A.
Lost Along the Way
CreateSpace, 2011
After Elizabeth Bennet Saunders finds her husband in bed with another woman, she sets out to discover herself. Helping are Georgiana Darcy and George Wickham and eventually, William Darcy.

☐ Cooper-Thumann, Rebecca A.
Longbourn State of Mind
CreateSpace, 2012
A contemporary story about the five Bennet sisters that takes place in Louisiana on Longbourn ranch. Everything is turned upside down when Darcy Accounting takes over the ranch's finances.

☐ Cox, Karen M.
1932
Meryton Press, 2010
Elizabeth Bennet leads a pampered life as the daughter of a university professor until adversity strikes. As she rebuilds a life for herself and her family she also discovers who she is.

☐ Cready, Gwyn
Seducing Mr. Darcy
Pocket Books, 2008
Flip Allison, a university professor, wakes up from a massage and she's in *Pride and Prejudice* liaising with Mr. Darcy. When she returns to present day life, she sees her actions have changed the events in *Pride and Prejudice*.

☐ Day, Summer
Pride & Princesses
CreateSpace, 2012
A contemporary young adult novel in which *Pride and Prejudice* meets *Emma*.

☐ Di Mattia, Sebastian
Starlight Over Pemberley
Sebastian Di Mattia, 2011
A road in Derbyshire intersects a path that appears at times that links the modern times to Regency England. A twenty-first century piano tuner follows the path and finds Georgiana Darcy.

☐ Di Mattia, Sebastian
There's Something About Mary Bennet
Sebastian Di Mattia, 2011
A follow-up to *Starlight Over Pemberley* featuring Mary Bennet as a wolf.

☑ Doornebos, Karen
Definitely Not Mr. Darcy
Berkley Trade, 2011
Chloe Parker is in her late 30s, divorced, a mother, running her own business and a huge Jane Austen and Regency fan. She auditions for a Jane Austen-inspired TV show that ends up being a reality dating show set in 1812.

☐ Eulberg, Elizabeth
Prom and Prejudice
Point, 2011
Lizzie and her best friend Jane attend the
Longbourn Academy where the prom is coming up.
The two meet Charles Bingley and Will Darcy.

☐ Fenton, Kate
Vanity and Vexation (also published as *Lions and Liquorice*)
St. Martin's Griffin, 2005
A modern interpretation in which the BBC is
making a movie of *Pride and Prejudice* in a small
village and the actors are living present day versions
of the story. In a twist, the Darcy and Bingley
characters are represented by women and Elizabeth
and Jane by men.

☑ Fielding, Helen
Bridget Jones's Diary
Penguin Books, 1996
This book follows a year in the life of Bridget Jones
and her suitors Mark Darcy and Daniel Cleaver.

☐ Frederick, Heather Vogel
Pies and Prejudice
Mother Daughter Book Club
Simon & Schuster Books for Young Readers, 2011
Emma's family announces they are moving to
England for a year, so the book club selects *Pride
and Prejudice* in honor of their adventure and keeps
up regular meetings via webcam.

☐ Harding, PM
Never Too Late for Love
Meryton Press, 2011
Darcy and Elizabeth were both in loveless
marriages. When both are in their fifties and have
lost their spouses, they meet for the first time.

☐ Hill, Georgia
Pursued by Love
E-scape Press, 2009
Perdita and Nick, stranded in a snowbound inn, are forced to reevaluate their first impressions of each other.

☐ Hubbard, Mandy
Prada and Prejudice
Razorbill, 2009
Callie, in London on a school trip, buys some Prada shoes, trips in them and wakes up in 1815. She meets Emily and her Darcy-like cousin Alex.

☐ James, Jenni
Pride and Popularity
Brigham Distributing, 2011
A high school adaptation about Chloe who is desperately trying to avoid the inevitable - falling for popular Taylor.

☐ Jeffers, Regina
Honor and Hope
Xlibris, 2008
A modern adaptation of *Pride and Prejudice* in which Darcy (a football player) and Elizabeth meet in college, move apart, then find each other again 6 years later.

☐ Kiely, Tracy
Murder at Longbourn
Minotaur Books, 2009
Elizabeth Parker travels to her great-aunt's bed-and-breakfast, the Inn at Longbourn, for a murder mystery party. There she encounters the Darcy-like Peter and an actual murder occurs.

☐ Kloss, Jennifer
Pride and Prejudice Revisited: Posers & Prom Dates
Amazon.com, 2011
Twins Jane and Lizzie Bennet meet Chaz and his
snobby sisters Caroline and Louisa, and their friend
Darcy Fitzwilliam as the story leads up to a prom.

☐ LaZebnik, Claire
Epic Fail
HarperTeen, 2011
Pride and Prejudice in high school as the new
principal's daughter mingles with the handsome,
privileged boys of her new school.

☐ Louise, Kara
Drive and Determination
Lulu.com, 2010
This book follows an interior designer who, at
her sister's wedding, clashes with the president of
Pemberleo Coffee. Later they meet again and things
go better for them.

☐ Nathan, Melissa
Pride, Prejudice and Jasmin Field (also published as
Acting Up)
Avon Books, 2001
Jasmin Field is an advice columnist who auditions
for a local production of *Pride and Prejudice* with a
Darcy-like director.

☐ Oakland, Ruth Phillips
My BFF
Meryton Press, 2009
Elizabeth is a professor at the Longbourn School
for the Arts in New York City where Georgiana
is an incoming student. Darcy meets Elizabeth to
discuss collaborating on a music education program
for underprivileged children.

☐ O'Rourke, Sally Smith
The Man Who Loved Jane Austen
Kensington, 2009
A woman researches letters she finds that were
sent between Jane Austen and a real-life Fitzwilliam
Darcy.

☐ O'Rourke, Sally Smith
Yours Affectionately, Jane Austen
Victorian Essence Press, 2012
A sequel to *The Man Who Loved Jane Austen.*

☐ Pastan, Rachel
This Side of Married
Viking Press, 2004
A novel of domestic manners that has been alluded
to as a modern day *Pride and Prejudice.* Evelyn Rubin
would like to see her three daughters happily
married however they don't always oblige her.

☐ Pattillo, Beth
Mr. Darcy Broke My Heart
GuidepostsBooks, 2010
Claire Prescott reads *First Impressions*, an early
version of *Pride and Prejudice*, which has a very
different love story for Elizabeth Bennet and starts
to question her own relationships.

☐ Pinkston, Tristi
Turning Pages
Walnut Springs Press, 2012
Blake is arrogant and engaged and has just gotten
Addie's promotion at the library. Addie learns the
library will be torn down. Should she fight for the
library and Blake?

☑ Potter, Alexandra
Me and Mr. Darcy
Ballantine Books, 2007
A twenty-something New York bookstore manager
blames her poor social life on Darcy since he
set the bar too high. She takes a tour of Darcy
territory, meets a journalist interviewing her group
and finds herself traveling through time.

☐ Raphael, Lev
Pride and Prejudice: The Jewess and the Gentile
Unknown, 2011
Lizzy Bennet has a Jewish mother, an attitude and
a lot to say about Darcy, who has a problem with
"Hebrews."

☐ Reed, Michele
Angel of the Centerfold
ShoeString Publishing, 2008
Dr. Jane Bennet is tired of being a good girl so
she spends a night out using the alias, Ariel, and
meets Charles Bingley who's also using an alias.
Meanwhile, her twin Elizabeth is having her own
romance with Darcy.

☐ Reynolds, Abigail
The Man Who Loved Pride & Prejudice (also published
as *Pemberley by the Sea*)
The Woods Hole Quartet
Sourcebooks Casablanca, 2010
Cassie and Calder are a couple just like Elizabeth
and Darcy whose romance is in jeopardy when their
families start to interfere. In a hope to save their
romance, Calder rewrites the two of them into *Pride
and Prejudice*.

☑ Rigaud, Heather Lynn
Fitzwilliam Darcy, Rock Star
Sourcebooks Landmark, 2011
Darcy is guitarist for a band called Slurry and
Elizabeth is lead singer for a band called Long
Borne Suffering. They meet on tour.

☐ Roberts, Belinda
Mr. Darcy Goes Overboard: A Tale of Tide & Prejudice
(also published as *Prawn and Prejudice*)
Sourcebooks Landmark, 2011
Yacht-owning Darcy is a catch for Mrs. Bennet's
daughters.

☐ Rushton, Rosie
Love, Lies and Lizzie
Jane Austen in 21st Century
Piccadilly Press, 2009
Mrs. Bennet inherits some money and moves the
family to a smart village where they're swept up in a
glamorous life. The girls discover that beneath the
surface lies intrigue and rivalries.

☐ Sadriani
Pick Me Up
Lulu.com, 2009
An inebriated Bingley phones Elizabeth Bennet for
a ride home for him, Darcy and cousin Richard.

☐ Shealy, Carissa
Lunatics and Lycanthropy
CreateSpace, 2011
A werewolf-inspired version of *Pride and Prejudice*.

☐ Simonsen, Mary Lydon
Searching for Pemberley (also published as *Pemberley Remembered*)
Sourcebooks Landmark, 2009
Maggie Joyce is an American who visits England in the late 1940s. She tours a house in Derbyshire whose former residents were the inspiration for Darcy and Elizabeth then meets and falls for Rob McAllister, another American who served in World War II.

☐ Simonsen, Mary Lydon
Mr. Darcy's Angel of Mercy: A Romance of the Great War
Quail Creek Publishing, 2011
After World War I, Darcy struggles with memories of the war while Elizabeth suppresses memories of her service in France with the Voluntary Aid Detachment. Darcy believes they have one memory in common of a special night in a French hospital ward.

☐ Simonsen, Mary Lydon
Darcy on the Hudson
Quail Creek Publishing, 2011
Darcy, Georgiana and Charles set sail to New York, each travelling for their own reason. Darcy's reason changes when he meets American Elizabeth while a possible second world war looms.

☐ Simonsen, Mary Lydon
Becoming Elizabeth Darcy
Quail Creek Publishing, 2011
Modern day Elizabeth has the flu and falls into a coma. When she wakes up, she's Elizabeth Bennet Darcy and she needs Darcy's help to get back to her own time.

☐ Simonsen, Mary Lydon
Darcy Goes to War
Quail Creek Publishing, 2012
A contemporary retelling of *Pride and Prejudice* set against World War II with Elizabeth and Darcy both part of the war effort.

☐ Smith, Debra White
First Impressions
The Austen Series
Harvest House, 2004
This is a Christian romance contemporary novel in which a lawyer and rancher clash and fall in love when starring in a local production based on *Pride and Prejudice.*

☐ Treglown, Tina L.
Finding Mr. Darcy
PulishAmerica, 2011
Emma Kennedy, armed with a vast knowledge of Jane Austen's works, believes she can find her own Mr. Darcy in Boston.

☐ Wegner, Ola
Realisations
CreateSpace, 2010
A time travel story in which a modern day student is hit by a car and wakes up in 1813 married to Darcy.

☐ Wells, Linda
Perfect Fit
CreateSpace, 2009
Darcy is burdened with maintaining his family's legacy and attempting to restore his sister's spirit after becoming the victim of Internet luring. Elizabeth is an author trying to move past a dominating former lover. They meet at a wedding, over a broken shoe.

OTHER

☐ Eland, Lindsay
Scones and Sensibility
Egmont USA, 2010
Polly's a romantic and one of her favorite books is
Pride and Prejudice. For the summer, she decides to
talk and act like a Jane Austen character.

☐ Measham, Donald
Jane Austen and the Polite Puzzle
Lulu.com, 2007
Young Jane Austen plays a card game and involves
readers in a discovery as they see the game
reenacted by Regency young ladies and their
governesses. *Pride and Prejudice* and *Persuasion* are
presented in social and historical context.

☐ Warren, Kate
Selected Works of Lady Indis Dress, Vol 1
Collier Bluff Books, 2008
This book includes outtakes, explanations and
limericks related to *Pride and Prejudice*.

☑ Webster, Emma Campbell
Lost in Austen: Create Your Own Jane Austen Adventure
(also published as *Being Elizabeth Bennet*)
Riverhead Trade, 2007
An interactive experience in which the reader
makes choices as Elizabeth Bennet and decides the
outcome of the book.

☑ White, TH
Darkness at Pemberley
V. Gollancz, 1932
A mystery that takes place at Pemberley. Does not
include characters from *Pride and Prejudice*.

NON-FICTION

☐ Arthur, Sarah
Dating Mr. Darcy: The Smart Girl's Guide to Sensible Romance
Thirsty, 2005
Insights and discussions of Jane Austen's stories and tips on gauging a man's "Darcy Potential."

☐ Birtwistle, Sue and Conklin, Susie
The Making of Pride & Prejudice
Penguin, 2003
Includes information on the making of the 1995 BBC production based on *Pride and Prejudice* with Jennifer Ehle and Colin Firth. It covers casting, the script, costumes, filming, post-production and more.

☐ Bottomer, Phyllis Ferguson
So Odd a Mixture: Along the Autistic Spectrum in Pride and Prejudice
Jessica Kingsley Publishers, 2007
This book studies eight characters in *Pride and Prejudice* who display autistic traits.

☐ Cartmell, Deborah
Screen Adaptations: Jane Austen's Pride and Prejudice: A Close Study of the Relationship between Text and Film
Methuen Drama, 2010
How the story and themes of *Pride and Prejudice* are interpreted in film adaptations.

☐ Chandler, Steve and Hill, Terrence N.
Two Guys Read Jane Austen
Robert Reed Publishers, 2008
The two guys take on *Pride and Prejudice* and *Mansfield Park*, reading and commenting on her novels and digressing into music, sports, and history.

☐ Crusie, Jennifer
Flirting with Pride and Prejudice: Fresh Perspectives on the Original Chick-Lit Masterpiece
Smart Pop, 2005
This collection of essays shows how *Pride and Prejudice* was a precursor to contemporary chick-lit.

☐ Fullerton, Susannah and Le Faye, Deirdre
A Dance with Jane Austen: How a Novelist and Her Characters Went to the Ball
Frances Lincoln, 2012
Describes the stages Jane Austen and her characters would go through preparing for and attending a Regency ball.

☐ Mattox, Brenda Sneathen
Elizabeth, Jane Austen's Pride & Prejudice: A Paper Doll
Dover Publications, 2000
This book includes a paper doll and clothes inspired by Elizabeth.

☐ Mattox, Brenda Sneathen
Pride and Prejudice Paper Dolls
Dover Publications, 1997
This book includes a paper doll and clothes inspired by *Pride and Prejudice*.

☐ Vaughn, Margaret
Tea with the Bennets
Allison & Alderson Associates, 1996
Recipes inspired by *Pride and Prejudice*.

SENSE AND SENSIBILITY

NEW VERSIONS

☐ Butler, Nancy and Liew, Sonny
Sense & Sensibility
Marvel Illustrated
Marvel , 2011
A graphic novel version of *Sense and Sensibility*.

RETELLINGS

☐ Grange, Amanda
Colonel Brandon's Diary
Berkley Trade, 2009
This book is a retelling of *Sense and Sensibility* from
Colonel Brandon's perspective.

☐ Greensmith, Jane
Imitations of Austen
Lulu.com, 2008
A collection of short stories that includes back
stories, sequels and what-ifs to Austen's novels.

☐ Nattress, Laurel Ann
*Jane Austen Made Me Do It: Original Stories Inspired by
Literature's Most Astute Observer of the Human Heart*
Ballantine Books, 2011
A collection of short stories inspired by Jane
Austen and her works.

☐ Simonsen, Mary Lydon
Elinor and Edward's Plans for Lucy Steele
Quail Creek Publishing, 2011
After falling in love, Elinor and Edward devise
a way to get Lucy to break her engagement to
Edward.

☑ Winters, Ben H. and Smith, Eugene
Sense and Sensibility and Sea Monsters
Quirk Books, 2009
Mr. Dashwood is eaten by a hammerhead shark and the Dashwood women are sent to Pestilent Island where they meet Sir John Middleton and squid-faced Colonel Brandon. Marianne is rescued from a giant octopus by Mr. Willoughby.

SEQUELS

☐ Aiken, Joan
Eliza's Daughter
St. Martin's Press, 1994
This book follows a minor character in *Sense and Sensibility* that is the illegitimate child of John Willoughby and Eliza Williams.

☑ Barrett, Julia
The Third Sister
Donald I. Fine Books, 1996
This book opens three years after the completion of *Sense and Sensibility* and focuses on Margaret Dashwood, the third sister, who is now 17 years old.

☐ Barrington, E. (aka Lily Adams Beck)
The Ladies! A Shining Constellation of Wit and Beauty
Unknown, 1922
A collection of short stories, one of which is called "The Darcys of Rosings Park." It takes place when the eldest Darcy child is seventeen and Elizabeth and Darcy have inherited Rosings. Also included are the Wickhams and Marianne and Willoughby.

☑ Brinton, Sybil G.
Old Friends and New Fancies: An Imaginary Sequel to the Novels of Jane Austen
Unknown, 1913
Considered the first Jane Austen fan-fiction story conceived, the author takes characters from all of Jane Austen's novels and weaves them into a "concluding" story.

☐ Brown, Francis
Margaret Dashwood, or Interference
John Lane, 1929
This book is a sequel to *Sense and Sensibility*.

☐ Caldwell, Jack
The Three Colonels: Jane Austen's Fighting Men
Sourcebooks Landmark, 2012
Bringing together two stories, Colonels Fitzwilliam, Buford (fiance of Caroline Bingley) and Brandon lead peaceful lives until the escape of Napoleon from exile.

☐ Collins, Rebecca Ann
Expectations of Happiness
Sourcebooks Landmark, 2011
A sequel to *Sense and Sensibility*.

☐ Gillespie, Jane
Brightsea
St. Martin's Press, 1987
This sequel focuses on Nancy Steele and Lucy Ferrars.

☐ Kaye-Smith, Sheila and Stern, G.B.
More Talk of Jane Austen
Cassell, 1950
This book includes speculation about the lives of those in Jane Austen's six complete novels.

☐ Odiwe, Jane
Willoughby's Return: A Tale of Almost Irresistible Temptation
Sourcebooks Landmark, 2009
This sequel picks up three years after Marianne and Colonel Brandon's wedding. Willoughby returns and Marianne deals with painful memories and uncertainty about the future.

☑ Tennant, Emma
Elinor and Marianne
Simon & Schuster, 1996
This book is a sequel to *Sense and Sensibility* in the form of correspondence between the Dashwood sisters.

☐ Ward, Eucharista
Rifts and Restorations: Margaret Dashwood's Story
Outskirts Press, 2010
Margaret Dashwood observes her sisters marriages and wonder whether she really desires marriage.

CONTEMPORARY

☐ Kiely, Tracy
Murder on the Bride's Side
Minotaur Books, 2010
Elizabeth Parker attends her friend's wedding in Richmond, Virginia, after which the bride's aunt turns up dead.

☐ Maddox, A.P.
Northland Cottage: Where the Heart Comes Home
Brighton Publishing, 2012
Mrs. Hathcock and her daughters, finding themselves in dire financial straits, leave the home they know and move to a new one. Details the daughters' trevails in modern day North Carolina.

☐ Pattillo, Beth
The Dashwood Sisters Tell All
GuidepostsBooks, 2011
Two sisters go on a walking tour of Jane Austen's
England and find what might be Jane Austen's long
lost diary. They discover that Jane and Cassandra
Austen inspired the characters Marianne and Elinor.

☐ Rushton, Rosie
Secrets of Love (also published as *The Dashwood Sisters'
Secrets of Love*)
Jane Austen in 21st Century
Piccadilly Press, 2005
Max Walker leaves his family then dies deep in debt.
The family moves to a seaside town and regroups.

☐ Schine, Cathleen
The Three Weissmanns of Westport
Farrar, Straus and Giroux, 2010
Betty Weissmann, dumped by her husband and
removed from her New York apartment, and
her two middle-aged daughters retreat to a beach
cottage in Westport, Connecticut.

☐ Schmais, Libby
The Perfect Elizabeth: A Tale of Two Sisters
St. Martin's Griffin, 2001
A modern-day *Sense and Sensibility* that follows two
sisters: Liza, a would-be poet and Bette, a graduate
student who deal with unemployment, infidelity,
medaling parents and more.

☐ Smith, Debra White
Reason and Romance
The Austen Series
Harvest House Publishers, 2004
This book is a contemporary Christian version of *Sense and Sensibility*. Ted arrives and Elaina is interested but thinks Ted won't be. Willis hints at engagement with Anna who is pleased but then Willis is called away.

☐ Ziegler, Jennifer
Sass & Serendipity
Delacorte Books for Young Readers, 2011
A contemporary young adult story of two very different sisters.

OTHER

☐ Schartz, Paula
Elinor and Marianne: Scenes from Sense & Sensibility
The Washington Court, 1990
Unknown.

NON-FICTION

☐ Hendricks, Donald
Elinor, Jane Austen's Sense & Sensibility: A Paper Doll
True Collectibles, 2000
This book includes a paper doll and clothes inspired by Elinor.

☑ James, Syrie
The Lost Memoirs of Jane Austen
William Morrow Paperbacks, 2007
Jane Austen's memoirs are discovered hundreds of
years after they were written and reveal the story
of a love affair between Jane Austen and a man
who inspires her work on the unfinished *Sense and
Sensibility.*

☐ Murnighan, Jack and Kelly, Maura
*Much Ado about Loving: What Our Favorite Novels
Can Teach You About Date Expectations, Not So-Great
Gatsbys, and Love in the Time of Internet Personals*
Free Press, 2012
Dating advice as found in classic novels including
Sense and Sensibility.

☐ Thompson, Emma
*The Sense and Sensibility Screenplay & Diaries: Bringing
Jane Austen's Novel to Film*
Newmarket Press, 2002
Emma Thompson's journal of the making of
the movie based on *Sense and Sensibility*, plus the
screenplay.

JANE AUSTEN

FICTION

☐ Aares, Pamela
Jane Austen and the Archangel
CreateSpace, 2012
The story of Jane Austen and her bad-boy
archangel, Michael Grace.

☐ Archer, Peter and Lawler, Jennifer
Bad Austen: The Worst Stories Jane Never Wrote
Adams Media, 2011
Compilation of contest entries for stories written
in Jane Austen's style on topics she would not have
written about.

☑ Ashford, Lindsay
The Mysterious Death of Miss Austen
Honno, 2011
A fictional account of Jane Austen's death that
starts with the real-life events that imply Jane
Austen died of arsenic poisoning.

☐ Aston, Elizabeth
Writing Jane Austen
Touchstone, 2010
Georgina Jackson has the opportunity to finish one
of Jane Austen's unfinished manuscripts. Because
she has never read anything by the author, she starts
reading Austen's novels and learns about herself in
the process.

☑ Barron, Stephanie
Jane and the Unpleasantness at Scargrave Manor
Being a Jane Austen Mystery
Bantam, 1996
First in a series of mysteries in which Jane Austen
is a sleuth.

☑ Barron, Stephanie
Jane and the Man of Cloth
Being a Jane Austen Mystery
Bantam, 1997
Second in a series in which Jane Austen is a sleuth.

☑ Barron, Stephanie
Jane and the Wandering Eye
Being a Jane Austen Mystery
Bantam, 1998
Third in a series in which Jane Austen is a sleuth.

☐ Barron, Stephanie
Jane and the Genius of the Place
Being a Jane Austen Mystery
Bantam, 1999
Fourth in a series in which Jane Austen is a sleuth.

☐ Barron, Stephanie
Jane and the Stillroom Maid
Being a Jane Austen Mystery
Bantam, 2000
Fifth in a series in which Jane Austen is a sleuth.

☐ Barron, Stephanie
Jane and the Prisoner of Wool House
Being a Jane Austen Mystery
Bantam, 2002
Sixth in a series in which Jane Austen is a sleuth.

☐ Barron, Stephanie
Jane and the Ghosts of Netley
Being a Jane Austen Mystery
Bantam, 2003
Seventh in a series in which Jane Austen is a sleuth.

☐ Barron, Stephanie
Jane and His Lordship's Legacy
Being a Jane Austen Mystery
Bantam, 2004
Eighth in a series in which Jane Austen is a sleuth.

☐ Barron, Stephanie
Jane and the Barque of Frailty
Being a Jane Austen Mystery
Bantam, 2007
Ninth in a series in which Jane Austen is a sleuth.

☐ Barron, Stephanie
Jane and the Madness of Lord Byron
Being a Jane Austen Mystery
Bantam, 2010
Tenth in a series in which Jane Austen is a sleuth.

☐ Barron, Stephanie
Jane and the Canterbury Tale
Being a Jane Austen Mystery
Bantam, 2011
Eleventh in a series in which Jane Austen is a sleuth.

☐ Bennett, Stuart
The Perfect Visit
Longbourn Press, 2011
Two bibliophiles go back in time - one to Jane
Austen's Regency England and the other to
Shakespeare's England - to save lost books.

☑ Bennett, Veronica
Cassandra's Sister: Growing Up Jane Austen
Candlewick, 2007
A historical novel about Jane Austen's childhood.

☐ Briggs, Laura
Christmas with Miss Austen
Pelican Book Group, 2011
Julia Allen is a waitress, a painter and moonlights
as Jane Austen on the weekends. Fleeing home one
night she is spied by book historian Eliot Weston.

☐ Brown, Laurie
What Would Jane Austen Do?
Sourcebooks Casablanca, 2009
This book follows Eleanor, a costume designer
working on a Jane Austen festival, who encounters
two ghost sisters who persuade Eleanor to travel
back in time to help prevent the duel that took their
brother's life.

☐ Connelly, Victoria
Mr. Darcy Forever
Sourcebooks, 2012
Sarah and Mia Castle are estranged sisters who fight
over the men in their lives. While attending the
annual Jane Austen Festival in Bath, England they
begin to make amends.

☑ Eckstut, Arielle and Ashton, Dennis
Pride and Promiscuity: The Lost Sex Scenes of Jane Austen
Touchstone, 2008
While staying at an English estate two amateur
Austen scholars come across manuscript pages
that contain omitted sex scenes from Jane Austen's
novels.

☐ Eugenides, Jeffrey
The Marriage Plot
Farrar, Straus and Giroux, 2011
The story of three college friends: Madeleine,
Mitchell and Leonard, during their senior year and
one year after graduation. Madeleine's senior thesis
is on the marriage plot in works by Jane Austen and
George Eliot.

☑ Ford, Michael Thomas
Jane Bites Back
Ballantine Books, 2009
Vampire Jane Austen is undead, over 200 years old,
an author and owner of a bookstore in upstate
New York.

☐ Ford, Michael Thomas
Jane Goes Batty
Ballantine Books, 2011
A follow-up to *Jane Bites Back*.

☐ Ford, Michael Thomas
Jane Vows Vengeance
Ballantine Books, 2012
A follow-up to *Jane Goes Batty*.

☑ Fowler, Karen Joy
The Jane Austen Book Club
Penguin Books, 2004
This book follows a book club as it takes on the
works of Jane Austen, and their own problems.

☐ Goodnight, Alyssa
Austentatious
Kensington, 2012
Nicola James finds a blank journal among a set of
Jane Austen book. When she writes in the journal,
Fairy Jane writes back.

☑ Hale, Shannon
Austenland
Bloomsbury USA, 2007
The journey of a 30-something single woman
for whom no man can measure up to Fitzwilliam
Darcy (specifically as embodied by Colin Firth) as
she travels to a resort where guests live like the
characters in Jane Austen novels.

☑ Hale, Shannon
Midnight in Austenland
Bloomsbury USA, 2012
The story of Charlotte Kinder's two-week vacation at Austenland.

☐ Hannon, Patrice
Dear Jane Austen: A Heroine's Guide to Life and Love
Plume, 2007
A series of letters in which Jane Austen gives advice and admonitions.

☑ Harrison, Cora
I was Jane Austen's Best Friend
Delacorte Books for Young Readers, 2010
A historical novel about Jane Austen's childhood.

☑ Harrison, Cora
Jane Austen Stole My Boyfriend
MacMillan Children's Books, 2011
A historical novel about Jane Austen's childhood.

☑ Izzo, Kim
The Jane Austen Marriage Manual
St. Martin's Griffin, 2012
Kate is a huge Jane Austen fan who gets a freelance writing assignment that asks, in modern times, is it possible to marry for money? Life mirroring her story, she finds herself in a situation of choosing between Mr. Rich and Mr. Right.

☑ James, Syrie
The Lost Memoirs of Jane Austen
William Morrow Paperbacks, 2007
Jane Austen's memoirs are discovered hundreds of years after they were written and reveal the story of a love affair between Jane Austen and a man who inspires her work on the unfinished *Sense and Sensibility*.

☐ James, Syrie
The Missing Manuscript of Jane Austen
Berkley Trade, 2012
Samantha finds a letter that appears to have been written by Jane Austen that references a missing manuscript. That sends her on a journey to find it.

☐ Jones, Cindy
My Jane Austen Summer: A Season in Mansfield Park
William Morrow Paperbacks, 2011
A down on her luck woman participates in a Jane Austen re-enacting festival.

☐ Kiely, Tracy
Murder Most Austen
Minotaur Books, 2012
Elizabeth Parker travels to the Jane Austen festival in Bath where an Austen scholar is murdered providing another mystery for Elizabeth to solve.

☐ Measham, Donald
Jane Austen and the Polite Puzzle
Lulu.com, 2007
Young Jane Austen plays a card game and involves readers in a discovery as they see the game reenacted by Regency young ladies and their governesses. *Pride and Prejudice* and *Persuasion* are presented in social and historical context.

☑ Moser, Nancy
Just Jane
Bethany House Publishers, 2007
A fictionalized biography of Jane Austen's life.

☐ Mullany, Janet
Jane and the Damned
William Morrow Paperbacks, 2010
At a ball, Jane is lured in by the damned and turned into a vampire.

☐ Mullany, Janet
Jane Austen: Blood Persuasion
William Morrow Paperbacks, 2011
A follow-up to *Jane and the Damned*, Jane has taken
the cure and is writing what will be her masterpiece
until once again, vampires descend.

☐ Nattress, Laurel Ann
*Jane Austen Made Me Do It: Original Stories Inspired by
Literature's Most Astute Observer of the Human Heart*
Ballantine Books, 2011
A collection of short stories inspired by Jane
Austen and her works.

☑ O'Rourke, Sally Smith
The Man Who Loved Jane Austen
Kensington, 2009
A woman researches letters she finds that were
sent between Jane Austen and a real-life Fitzwilliam
Darcy.

☑ Pattillo, Beth
Jane Austen Ruined My Life
GuidepostsBooks, 2009
Emma Grant has a score to settle with Jane
Austen whose novels taught Emma to believe in
happy endings which are short in Emma's life. She
travels to England after being notified by a woman
claiming to have a collection of lost Austen letters.

☐ Pitkeathly, Jill
Cassandra & Jane
Harper Paperbacks, 2008
A fictionalized biography of Jane Austen from her
sister Cassandra's point of view.

☑ Pitkeathly, Jill
Dearest Cousin Jane
Harper Paperbacks, 2010
Jane Austen's cousin, Countess Eliza de Feuillide, is
the focus of this book.

☑ Rigler, Laurie Viera
Confessions of a Jane Austen Addict
Plume, 2007
The story of Courtney Stone, a modern day
American career woman recovering from a breakup,
wakes up one morning as Jane Mansfield, a lady in
nineteenth century England and how she copes in
her new world.

☐ Rigler, Laurie Viera
Rude Awakenings of a Jane Austen Addict
Plume, 2009
Follow-up to *Confessions of a Jane Austen Addict*,
this is the story of Jane Mansfield, a gentleman's
daughter from Regency England, who wakes up in
Courtney Stone's modern day life in Los Angeles.

☐ Santini, Rosemarie
*Sex & Sensibility: The Adventures of a Jane Austen
Addict*
Saint Books, 2005
Lizzie Parsons is a Manhattan film reviewer who
meets regularly with a Jane Austen club where
members discuss living by the standards of
behavior set by Jane Austen.

☐ Shulman, Polly
Enthusiasm
Speak, 2007
Best friends Julia and Ashleigh are both Jane
Austen fans and looking for romance. They crash a
boys' prep school dance in search of their own Mr.
Darcy.

☐ Solender, Elsa A.
Jane Austen in Love: An Entertainment
Unknown, 2012
Jane Austen's love life is the subject of this fictional story based on known details of her life.

☐ Southard, Scott D.
A Jane Austen Daydream
CreateSpace, 2012
Jane Austen's live as a novel in which she meets with gypsies then sets out to find her soul mate.

☐ Various
Dancing with Mr. Darcy: Stories Inspired by Jane Austen and Chawton House
Honno Welsh Womens Press, 2009
An anthology of the winning entries for the Jane Austen Short Story Award.

☐ Willig, Lauren
The Mischief of the Mistletoe
Pink Carnation
Dutton Adult, 2011
Turnip Fitzhugh visits his sister at boarding school and encounters school mistress Arabella Dempsey and her best friend Jane Austen.

☐ Wilson, Barbara Ker
The Lost Years of Jane Austen (also published as *Jane Austen in Australia* and *Antipodes Jane*)
Ulysses Press, 2008
Jane Austen's letters and diaries may have been destroyed by her sister Cassandra to either hide a family scandal or a failed romance. This fictionalized biography begins with an actual event, the arrest of Jane's aunt, Mrs. Leigh Perrot, and follows Jane's journey to a prison colony in Australia.

☐ Winslow, Shannon
For Myself Alone
Heather Ridge Arts, 2012
The story of Josephine Walker, a nineteenth century young woman, who comes into a fortune, but wants to be loved for herself. Jane Austen quotations run throughout the book.

NON-FICTION

☐ [No Author]
The Jane Austen Companion to Love
Sourcebooks, 2009
Jane Austen's thoughts on love with four-color illustrations.

☐ [No Author]
The Jane Austen Companion to Life
Sourcebooks, 2010
Quotations and watercolor illustrations inspired by Jane Austen's novels.

☐ Adams, Carol J., Gesch, Kelly and Buchanan, Douglas
The Bedside, Bathtub & Armchair Companion to Jane Austen
Continuum, 2008
Contains summaries of Austen's novels, information on topics such as carriages, food, movie adaptations, maps, puzzles and quizzes.

☐ Adams, Jennifer
Remarkably Jane: Notable Quotations on Jane Austen
Gibbs Smith, 2009
One hundred quotations on Jane Austen and her writing from other authors, critics and intellectuals, plus those involved in adaptations of her novels.

☐ Barchas, Janine
Matters of Fact in Jane Austen: History, Location, and Celebrity
The Johns Hopkins University Press, 2012
This book describes Jane Austen as a historian and outlines the links between celebrities of her time and characters in her novels.

☐ Bedford-Pierce, Sophia
Jane Austen's Little Instruction Book
Peter Pauper Press, 1995
A collection of Jane Austen quotations.

☐ Black, Maggie and Le Faye, Deirdre
The Jane Austen Cookbook
McClelland & Stewart, 2002
Set within the context of Jane Austen's social and domestic history, this book includes information on Austen's friends, novels, letters, social life and customs plus recipes adapted for the modern kitchen.

☐ Blakemore, Erin
The Heroine's Bookshelf: Life Lessons, from Jane Austen to Laura Ingalls Wilder
Harper Perennial, 2011
Strong literary characters such as Elizabeth Bennet, Jane Eyre and Laura Ingalls Wilder are highlighted and put forth as models for modern women to live their lives with intelligence and grace.

☐ Bolton, Leslie
The Jane Austen Miscellany
Sourcebooks, 2006
Includes facts about Jane Austen's life, quotations about her and her work, quotations from her works and letters, profiles of her characters and suggestions for further reading.

☑ Brownstein, Rachel M.
Why Jane Austen?
Columbia University Press, 2011
Information on why Jane Austen is read and adapted.

☐ Byrde, Penelope
Jane Austen Fashion
Moonrise Press, 2008
An illustrated guide to fashion in Jane Austen's time.

☐ Carson, Susannah
A Truth Universally Acknowledged: 33 Great Writers on Why We Read Jane Austen
Random House Trade Paperbacks, 2010
Essays by various authors on Austen's popularity.

☐ Dabundo, Laura
The Marriage of Faith: Christianity in Jane Austen and William Wordsworth
Mercer University Press, 2012
Information on how the religious background of Jane Austen and William Wordsworth influenced their work.

☐ Danielson, Diane K. and Pollak, Lindsey
Savvy Gal's Guide to Online Networking (Or, What Would Jane Austen Do?)
Booklocker.com, 2007
Applying Jane Austen for the businesswoman, this book offers advice and etiquette advice for building professional relationships through email and social media.

☑ Deresiewicz, William
A Jane Austen Education: How Six Novels Taught Me about Love, Friendship, and the Things That Really Matter
Penguin Press, 2011
The author highlights the life lessons in Jane Austen's novels he learns as he progresses from student to married man.

☐ Dickson, Rebecca
Jane Austen: An Illustrated Treasury
Metro Books, 2008
All things Jane Austen including removable memorabilia such as handwritten letters and drafts.

☐ Downing, Sarah-Jane
Fashion in the Time of Jane Austen
Shire, 2010
A guide to Regency-era women's and men's clothing.

☐ Dryden, Robert and Diaz, Robyn
Jane Austen for Beginners
For Beginners, 2012
Explores Austen's intention for her novels including addressing money, marriage and class movement.

☐ Enright, Dominique
The Wit & Wisdom of Jane Austen: Quotes from Her Novels, Letters & Diaries
Ulysses Press, 2008
A collection of Jane Austen's insights and social commentary on universal human traits.

☐ Forest, Jennifer
Jane Austen's Sewing Box
Murdoch Books, 2009
A look at Jane Austen's novels and letters and the arts and design described within. Includes illustrated instructions for related craft projects.

☐ Fullerton, Susannah and Hill, Reginald
Jane Austen and Crime
Jones Books, 2006
An examination of crime and criminals in Jane
Austen's time.

☐ Fullerton, Susannah and Le Faye, Deirdre
*A Dance with Jane Austen: How a Novelist and Her
Characters Went to the Ball*
Frances Lincoln, 2012
Describes the stages Jane Austen and her characters
would go through preparing for and attending a
Regency ball.

☑ Fullerton, Susannah
*Celebrating Pride and Prejudice: 200 Years of Jane
Austen's Masterpiece*
Voyageur Press, 2013,
This book celebrates what makes *Pride and Prejudice*
a masterpiece that has inspired numerous books
and films.

☑ Hannon, Patrice
*101 Things You Didn't Know about Jane Austen: The
Truth about the World's Most Intriguing Romantic Literary
Heroine*
Adams Media, 2007
This book includes over one hundred facts about
Jane Austen's life and works.

☑ Harman, Claire
Jane's Fame: How Jane Austen Conquered the World
Henry Holt, 2010
A biography of Jane Austen and commentary on
her lasting influence.

☑ Henderson, Lauren
Jane Austen's Guide to Dating
Hyperion, 2005
Provides information on navigating the dating
scene through examples of Austen's characters.

☐ Horozewski, Melissa
*Austentatious Crochet: 36 Contemporary Designs from the
World of Jane Austen*
Running Press, 2011
Crochet projects inspired by Jane Austen's novels.

☑ Ivins, Holly
Jane Austen Pocket Bible
White Ladder Press, 2010
A guide to Jane Austen's novels and her times
including Regency manners, inheriting, the class
system and finding a husband.

☐ Johnson, Claudia L.
Jane Austen's Cults and Cultures
University of Chicago Press, 2012
An account of Jane Austen's lasting appeal to
readers, critics, scholars and fans.

☐ Jones, Hazel
Jane Austen and Marriage
Continuum, 2009
A look at how marriage is depicted in Jane Austen's
life and books.

☐ Kantor, Elizabeth
The Jane Austen Guide to Happily Ever After
Regnery Publishing, 2012
Through the examples of Jane Austen heroines,
modern women learn lessons on dating, love,
relationships and sex.

☐ Lane, Maggie
Jane Austen Quiz & Puzzle Book
Abson Books, 1982
A gamebook with Jane Austen-themed puzzles and quizzes.

☐ Lane, Maggie
Jane Austen's England
Robert Hale, 1995
Describes Austen's places in English towns and the countryside, from her life and books.

☑ Lane, Maggie
Jane Austen's World: The Life and Times of England's Most Popular Author
Carlton Books, 2005
A look at the historical and social times during which Jane Austen wrote her novels.

☐ Lane, Maggie
Jane Austen and Food
Hambledon Continuum, 2007
This book offers information on food history in England, food in Jane Austen's novels and Austen's own attitude towards food.

☐ Le Faye, Deirdre
Jane Austen: The World of her Novels
Harry N. Abrams, 2002
This book provides context to Jane Austen's novels with information on social customs, sanitation and more, plus biographical information on Jane Austen.

☑ Le Faye, Deirdre
Jane Austen's Letters
Oxford University Press, 2011
A collection of Jane Austen's letters and information on her life and family.

☐ MacDonald, Gina and MacDonald, Andrew
Jane Austen on Screen
Cambridge University Press, 2003
This book discusses transferring Jane Austen's works into film.

☐ Michon, Cathryn and Norris, Pamela
Jane Austen's Little Advice Book
Harpercollins, 1996
This book contains Austen quotations and information about her and the times in which she lived.

☐ Monaghan, David, Hudelet, Ariane and Wiltshire, John
The Cinematic Jane Austen: Essays on the Filmic Sensibility of the Novels
McFarland, 2009
This book argues for an approach to film adaptations necessary for Jane Austen's works that focuses their auditory and visual dimensions.

☐ Moore, Constance
Jane Austen on Love and Romance
Summersdale, 2010
Using Jane Austen's writing, a guide to flirting, courtship and love.

☐ Mullan, John
What Matters in Jane Austen?: Twenty Crucial Puzzles Solved
Bloomsbury Press, 2013
Provides information on Jane Austen's world providing context for her novels.

☐ Mullen, Shawna
The Wisdom of Jane Austen
Citadel, 2003
A collection of Jane Austen's insights.

☐ Newgarden, Anne
Becoming Jane Austen: The Wit and Wisdom of Jane Austen
Miramax, Movie Tie In, 2007
This book is inspired by the movie of the same name and includes information about Austen and some of her well known quotations.

☐ Olsen, Kirstin
Cooking with Jane Austen
Greenwood, 2005
Recipes for dishes featured in Jane Austen's novels plus additional information about the dishes.

☐ Olsen, Kirstin
All Things Austen: An Encyclopedia of Austen's World
Greenwood, 2005
An encyclopedia of Jane Austen's world as seen through her literature.

☐ Parrill, Sue
Jane Austen on Film and Television: A Critical Study of the Adaptations
McFarland & Company, 2002
A history of film and television adaptations of Jane Austen's books.

☐ Pool, Daniel
What Jane Austen Ate and Charles Dickens Knew: From Fox Hunting to Whist - The Facts of Daily Life in Nineteenth-Century England
Touchstone, 1994
A guide to daily British life in nineteenth century England. Includes information on clothing, manners, marriage, money and transportation and a glossary of commonly used words and phrases.

☑ Ray, Joan Klingel
Jane Austen for Dummies
For Dummies, 2006
Includes information on Jane Austen's life and
works and their impact on our culture.

☐ Reef, Catherine
Jane Austen: A Life Revealed
Clarion Books, 2011
A biography of Jane Austen geared for young adult
readers.

☑ Rodi, Robert
*Bitch in a Bonnet: Reclaiming Jane Austen from the Stiffs,
the Snobs, the Simps and the Saps* (Volume 1)
CreateSpace, 2012
Bitch in a Bonnet makes the case that Jane Austen was
not just a quaint woman's writer but rather was a
subversive satirist.

☐ Ross, Josephine
Jane Austen: A Companion
Rutgers University Press, 2006
A general guide to Jane Austen and her world. It
provides information on the books considered
classics when Austen's novels were first published,
architecture and decor, fashion, relationships, class
and the military.

☐ Ross, Josephine and Webb, Henrietta
*Jane Austen's Guide to Good Manners: Compliments,
Charades & Horrible Blunders*
Bloomsbury, 2006
This guide is written in the form of letters between
Jane Austen and her niece Anna about the manners
of the day.

☐ Rowlatt, Bee and Witwit, May
Talking About Jane Austen in Baghdad: The True Story of an Unlikely Friendship
Penguin Global, 2011
May is Iraqi, a lecturer in English and lives in Baghdad. Bee is a mother of three living in London. An email brings them together and they build a friendship that transcends cultural, religious and age differences.

☐ Smith, Amy
All Roads Lead to Austen: A Year-long Journey with Jane
Sourcebooks, 2012
A recounting of the author's journey organizing Jane Austen book clubs in Central and South American countries.

☐ Smith, Debra White
What Jane Austen Taught Me about Love and Romance
Harvest House Publishers, 2007
The author of a series of contemporary Christian novels based on Austen's novels explains how the themes of Jane Austen's novels parallel scriptural imperatives about love.

☐ Smith, Lori
A Walk with Jane Austen: A Journey into Adventure, Love and Faith
WaterBrook Press, 2007
A chronicle of the author's journeys to England to see the places Jane Austen lived in and wrote about.

☐ Smith, Lori
The Jane Austen Guide to Life: Thoughtful Lessons for the Modern Woman
skirt!, 2012
Through Jane Austen's books, modern women get relationship advice.

☑ Smith, Rebecca
Miss Jane Austen's Guide to Modern Life's Dilemmas: Answers to Your Most Burning Questions about Life, Love, Happiness (and What to Wear) from the Great Novelist Herself
Tarcher, 2012
Answers to today's dilemmas drawn from Jane Austen's novels, letters, and unpublished writings.

☑ Spence, Jon
Becoming Jane Austen: The True Love Story That Inspired the Classic Novels
MJF Publishers, 2003
A biography of Jane Austen.

☑ Sullivan, Margaret C.
The Jane Austen Handbook: A Sensible yet Elegant Guide to Her World
Quirk Books, 2007
Instructions for navigating Regency life with explanations of the English class system, dressing, running a house, throwing a party and more.

☐ Sutherland, John and Le Faye, Deirdre
So You Think you Know Jane Austen: A Literary Quizbook
Oxford University Press, 2005
A series of quizzes testing the reader's knowledge of Jane Austen's novels. Four different levels of quizzes are included.

☐ The Puzzle Society
Pocket Posh Jane Austen: 100 Puzzles & Quizzes
Andrews McMeel Publishing, 2011
A game book with Jane Austen-themed puzzles including word search, crosswords, and more.

☐ Troost, Linda and Greenfield, Sayre
Jane Austen in Hollywood
The University Press of Kentucky, 1998
Essays on how Jane Austen's novels have been
adapted for film and television.

☐ Tyler, Natalie
*The Friendly Jane Austen: A Well-Mannered Introduction
to a Lady of Sense and Sensibility*
Penguin, 2001
Includes information on Austen's works, movie
adaptations and period society. Includes quizzes,
illustrations, quotations and interviews.

☐ Wells, Juliette
Everybody's Jane: Austen in the Popular Imagination
Continuum, 2012
A study of the appropriations of Jane Austen's
work.

☐ Wilson, Kim
Tea with Jane Austen
Jones Books, 2004
Information about buying, preparing, serving and
drinking tea in Jane Austen's day.

☐ Wilson, Kim
In the Garden with Jane Austen
Jones Books, 2008
An illustrated look at the gardens, parks and estates
of Regency England. It includes photographs,
history, biographical information, drawings,
instructions on creating an English garden and sites
mentioned in the book.

☐ Woolsey, Steffany
Jane Austen Devotional
Thomas Nelson, 2012
Excerpts from Jane Austen's books with
corresponding devotional thoughts and Scripture.

MOVIES

EMMA

☐ **Emma**
BBC, 1948
Judy Campbell and Ralph Michael

☐ **Emma**
NBC, 1954
Felicia Montealegre and Peter Cookson

☐ **Emma**
BBC, 1960
Diana Fairfax and Paul Daneman

☐ **Emma**
CBS, 1960
Nancy Wickwire and Unknown

☑ **Emma**
BBC, 1972
Doran Goodwin and John Carson

☑ **Clueless**
Paramount Pictures, 1995
Alicia Silverstone and Paul Rudd
A contemporary adaption of *Emma*.

☑ **Emma**
Meridian Broadcasting, 1996
Kate Beckinsale and Mark Strong

☑ **Emma**
Miramax Films, 1996
Gwyneth Paltrow and Jeremy Northam

☐ **Emma**
BBC, 2009
Romola Garai and Jonny Lee Miller

MANSFIELD PARK

☑ Mansfield Park
ITV, 1983
Sylvestra Le Touzel and Nicholas Farrell

☑ Mansfield Park
BBC, 1999
Frances O'Connor and Jonny Lee Miller

☑ Mansfield Park
PBS, 2008
Billie Piper and Blake Ritson

NORTHANGER ABBEY

☑ Northanger Abbey
BBC, 1986
Katharine Schlesinger and Peter Firth

☐ **Pup Fiction**
Big Feats! Entertainment, 1997
An episode of the Wishbone television series.

☑ Northanger Abbey
ITV, 2007
Felicity Jones and JJ Feild

PERSUASION

☐ **Persuasion**
BBC, 1960
Daphne Slater and Paul Daneman

☐ **Persuasion**
Granada Television, 1971
Ann Firbank and Bryan Marshall

Persuasion
Sony Pictures, 1995
Amanda Root and Ciaran Hinds

Bridget Jones: The Edge of Reason
Universal Pictures, 2004
Renee Zellweger and Colin Firth
An adaptation of the book, *Bridget Jones: The Edge of Reason*.

Persuasion
PBS, 2008
Sally Hawkins and Rupert Penry-Jones

PRIDE AND PREJUDICE

☐ **Pride and Prejudice**
BBC, 1938
Curigwen Lewis and Andrew Osborn

Pride and Prejudice
Loew's, 1940
Greer Garson and Laurence Olivier

☐ **Pride and Prejudice**
NBC, 1949
Madge Evans and John Baragrey

☐ **Pride and Prejudice**
BBC, 1952
Daphne Slater and Peter Cushing

☐ **Pride and Prejudice**
BBC, 1958
Jane Downs and Alan Badel

☐ **Pride and Prejudice**
BBC, 1967
Celia Bannerman and Lewis Fiander

☑ Pride and Prejudice
BBC, 1980
Elizabeth Garvie and David Rintoul

☑ Pride and Prejudice
BBC, 1995
Jennifer Ehle and Colin Firth

☐ Furst Impressions
Big Feats! Entertainment, 1996
An episode of the Wishbone television series.

☐ Beyond a Joke
Unknown, 1997
An episode of the Red Dwarf series in which the crew spend time in a virtual reality version of Pride and Prejudice Land in Jane Austen World.

☑ Bridget Jones's Diary
Miramax Films, 2001
Renee Zellweger and Colin Firth
An adaptation of the book, *Bridget Jones's Diary.*

☐ Pride and Prejudice: A Latter Day Comedy
Best Boy Pictures, 2003
Kam Heskin and Orlando Seale
A contemporary Mormon-influenced film adaptation of *Pride and Prejudice.*

☑ Bride and Prejudice
Bride Productions, 2004
Aishwarya Rai and Martin Henderson
A contemporary Bollywood film version of *Pride and Prejudice.*

☑ Pride and Prejudice
Focus Features, 2005
Keira Knightley and Matthew Macfadyen

☑ **Lost in Austen** (alternate title – Inside Austen)
Mammoth Screen, 2008
Jemima Rooper and Elliot Cowan
An adaptation of the book, *Lost in Austen*.

☐ **Pride and Prejudice and Zombies: Dawn of the Dreadfuls**
Dirty Robber, 2010
Anabella Casanova and Cameron Cash

☐ **A Modern Pride and Prejudice**
PaperCut Productions, 2011
Maia Petee and Caleb Grusing
A contemporary remake of *Pride and Prejudice*.

SENSE AND SENSIBILITY

☐ **Sense and Sensibility**
NBC, 1950
Madge Evans and Cloris Leachman

☐ **Sense and Sensibility**
BBC, 1971
Joanna David and Ciaran Madden

☑ **Sense and Sensibility**
BBC, 1981
Irene Richard and Tracey Childs

☑ **Sense and Sensibility**
Columbia Pictures, 1995
Emma Thompson and Kate Winslet

☑ **Sense and Sensibility**
BBC, 1995
Hattie Morahan and Charity Wakefield

☐ **Kandukondain Kandukondain** (alternate title – I Have Found It)
Sri Surya Films, 2000
Tabu and Aishwarya Rai
A contemporary Bollywood version of *Sense and Sensibility*.

☐ **Scents and Sensibility**
Silver Peak Productions, 2011
Ashley Williams and Marla Sokoloff
A contemporary remake of *Sense and Sensibility*.

☐ **From Prada to Nada** (alternate title – Sense and Sensibilidad)
Odd Lot Entertainment, 2011
Camilla Belle and Alexa Vega
A Latina film version of *Sense and Sensibility* set in contemporary Los Angeles.

JANE AUSTEN

☑ **Jane Austen in Manhattan**
Merchant Ivory Productions, 1980
Anne Baxter and Robert Powell
Film theatre companies compete to produce versions of a Jane Austen play.

☐ **The Real Jane Austen**
Unknown, 2002
Anna Chancellor and Gillian Kearney
A biography of Jane Austen.

☑ **The Jane Austen Book Club**
Sony Pictures, 2007
Ensemble cast
A film adaptation of the book *The Jane Austen Book Club*.

☑ Becoming Jane
HanWay Films, 2007
Anne Hathaway and James McAvoy
A biography of Jane Austen.

☑ Miss Austen Regrets
BBC, 2008
Olivia Williams and Samuel Roukin
A biography of Jane Austen.

AUTHOR INDEX

Aares, Pamela, 118
Adams, Aimee E., 66
Adams, Alexa, 39
Adams, Carol J., 128
Adams, Jennifer, 39, 128
Adkins, Samantha, 66
Adriani, Susan, 40
Aidan, Pamela, 38, 40
Aiken, Joan, 10, 19, 66, 111
Aitken, Virginia, 66
Allen, Dorothy, 18
Altman, Marsha, 67-68
Aminadra, Karen, 68
Anderson, Winter K., 91
Andi, Beverley, 91
Angelini, Sara, 92
Angell, Lavinia, 40
Archer, Juliet, 14, 32
Archer, Peter, 118
Armstrong, Amy, 41
Arrasmith, Patrick, 38
Arthur, Sarah, 107
Ashford, Lindsay, 118
Ashton, Dennis, 121
Aston, Elizabeth, 68-69, 118
Atchia, Paula, 19
Austen, Jan, 92-93
Austen-Leigh, Joan, 10, 12
Avery, Aimee, 41, 66, 93
Ayers, John D., 69
Aylmer, Janet, 41
Bader, Marilyn, 70
Bader, Ted, 70
Baker, Helen, 30, 70
Balogh, Mary, 32
Barchas, Janine, 129
Barrett, Julia, 70, 111
Barrington, E., 70, 111

Barron, Stephanie, 118-120
Baxley, M.K., 41, 93
Bebris, Carrie, 71
Beck, Lily Adams, see Barrington, E.
Beckford, Grania, 28
Becton, Jennifer, 72
Bedford-Pierce, Sophia, 129
Benneton, Nina, 94
Bennett, Stuart, 120
Bennett, Veronica, 120
Berdoll, Linda, 72
Bianchi, Moira, 94
Billington, Rachel, 12
Birchall, Diana, 12, 72
Birtwistle, Sue, 15, 07
Black, Maggie, 129
Blakemore, Erin, 129
Bligard, Carey, see Pierson, C. Allyn
Bloom, Annabella, see Pillow, Michelle
Bolton, Leslie, 129
Bonavia-Hunt, D.A., 73
Bottomer, Phyllis Ferguson, 107
Brant, Marilyn, 94
Briggs, Laura, 94, 121
Brinton, Sybil G., 13, 20, 21, 30, 73, 112
Brocklehurst, Judith, 73
Brokow, Andrea Marie, 94
Brooke-Rose, Christine, 15
Brown, Francis, 20, 112
Brown, Laurie, 121
Brown, Mary Calhoun, 95

SUBJECT INDEX

Fashion

Dating, Advice and Manners

Fantasy, Paranormal, Occult, etc.

Time Travel

Mystery

Passion

Religion

Vampires, Zombies, Werewolves, etc.

Quizzes and Puzzles

JANE AUSTEN JUNKIE

CHARACTER INDEX

Emma

The Campbells
Jane Fairfax, 12

The Eltons
Mrs. Elton in America, 12
Truth and Rumor, 13

Frank Churchill
Lovers' Perjuries: or, the Clandestine Courtship of Jane
    Fairfax and Frank Churchill, 11

Jane Fairfax
Jane Fairfax, 12
Jane Fairfax: The Secret Story of the Second Heroine in
    Jane Austen's Emma, 10
The Journal of Miss Jane Fairfax, 11
Lovers' Perjuries: or, the Clandestine Courtship of Jane
    Fairfax and Frank Churchill, 11

Knightley
George Knightley, Esquire: Charity Envieth Not, 10
George Knightley, Esquire: Lend Me Leave, 10
Mr. Knightley's Diary, 11

The Martins
Truth and Rumor, 13

Mrs. Goddard
Later Days at Highbury, 12
A Visit to Highbury/Another View of Emma, 10

Mansfield Park
Edmund Bertram
Edmund Bertram's Diary, 18

Henry Crawford
Miss Abigail's Part, or Version and Diversion, 19

Julia Bertram
Miss Abigail's Part, or Version and Diversion, 19

Mary Crawford
Murder at Mansfield Park, 18

Tom Bertram
The Reluctant Baronet, 20

The Wards
The Youngest Miss Ward, 19

Northanger Abbey
Henry Tilney
Henry Tilney's Diary, 24

Persuasion
Anne Elliott
Anne Elliot, a New Beginning, 30

Elizabeth Elliott
Mercy's Embrace: Elizabeth Elliot's Story Book 1 - So
    Rough a Course, 31
Mercy's Embrace: Elizabeth Elliot's Story Book 2 - So
    Lively a Chase, 31
Mercy's Embrace: Elizabeth Elliot's Story Book 3 - The
    Lady Must Decide, 31

Mrs. Clay
Connivance, 30
Sir Willy, 31

Wentworth
Captain Wentworth Home from the Sea, 30
Captain Wentworth's Diary, 28

Sense and Sensibility

the end

CPSIA information can be obtained at www.ICGtesting.com
Printed in the USA
LVOW12s1933140514

385785LV00027B/1005/P